Building *the* Winning Team

MOVING ON TO MATURITY

ALTON GARRISON

Developed by the Sunday School
Promotion & Training Department

Gospel Publishing House
Springfield, Missouri
02-0699

This is the third in a series of five books dealing with the We Build People model of discipleship. Each of the books is written to give you a deeper insight into each of the four bases of the model. The baseball diamond illustration mentioned in this book is adapted from materials developed by Pastor Rick Warren of Saddleback Church for his book *The Purpose Driven Church: Growth Without Compromising Your Message & Mission* and is used by permission of Zondervan Publishing House.

All Scripture quotations, unless otherwise indicated, are taken from the HOLY BIBLE, NEW INTERNATIONAL VERSION®; NIV®. Copyright ©1973, 1978, 1984 by International Bible Society. Used by permission of Zondervan Publishing House. All rights reserved.

Library of Congress Cataloging Card Number 98-73830
International Standard Book Number 0-88243-699-6
Printed in the United States of America

Contents

Preface

"Come and follow Me," Jesus said to His disciples, "and I will make you fishers of men." His call carried a mutual commitment: As the Twelve committed themselves to His teaching, Jesus committed himself to their development. In the months that followed, He taught them about God and about themelves. Throughout His earthly ministry, they talked and prayed and learned together.

When Jesus returned to the Father, He left behind a core of disciples who would make an eternal impact on their world. In His final instructions He mandated that they continue what they had seen Him begin: They were to disciple others. This is still the church's mission.

A key facet of discipleship is obedience to the teachings of Christ. Since one cannot obey what one does not know or understand, instruction in God's Word is essential to spiritual growth. Among the people in our congregations are new Christians who are just starting out on the path of discipleship. Others may have been Christians for a time, but they do not observe the disciplines of a disciple, such as prayer; Bible study; stewardship of time, talent, and resources; and sharing one's faith with others. Are we providing opportunities for them to develop in their spiritual experience so they will reflect Christ's teachings in their lives and reproduce that pattern in others? Are we encouraging them to make a commitment to maturity?

In the *We Build People* model, this commitment to maturity is Base 2. After bringing people to a personal relationship with Christ through salvation and with the church body through friendship, the church's role is to instruct them in the Word and to help them develop a prayer life. The church can do this best by (1) enrolling people in a discipleship group, (2) teaching spiritual disciplines, (3) establishing mentoring relationships, and (4) modeling a biblical lifestyle.

As the church develops these four habits and keeps its commitment to instruct, people are better able to make and keep their commitment to maturity.

The church that instructs will be strong, stable, and effective. It will develop members who are true disciples—discovering and using their ministry gifts in service to Christ and the church.

Building the Winning Team is a second-base study. It is especially significant to Sunday school teachers and small-group leaders. Alton Garrison examines how church's educational ministries provide the setting and instruction to lead disciples to full maturity in Christ. He describes the processes by which instruction can best happen and provides a practical means of evaluating educational ministries. His counsel grows out of years of pastoring and commitment to helping people grow in their spiritual maturity.

Christian education is not optional. By definition a disciple is a learner, and learning is a lifelong process. *Building the Winning Team* is an opportunity for every leader to reexamine the priority of teaching in the church. It is a challenge to develop quality experiences that will encourage every believer to become part of a discipleship group and to grow into a mature disciple of Jesus Christ.

Introduction

The Law of Instruction Defined

The Law of Instruction says: A disciple-making church provides an intentional process of Bible-based, life-centered instruction that contributes to the lifelong learning and development of believers.

Four Habits of Disciple-Making Churches

To fulfill the commitment to instruct developing believers into disciples, the church must focus on four habits:

ENROLL IN A DISCIPLESHIP GROUP

Enroll people in a discipleship group. This is foundational to all effective discipling. The group is the best place to learn, develop, and practice the principles of Christian living. People need a group and accountability to help them increase in commitment and spiritual growth. In the nurturing group they find and fulfill God's design for their lives. They gain a sense of belonging, and they can develop their unique identities.

TEACH SPIRITUAL DISCIPLINES

The habit of teaching spiritual disciplines is developed through understanding what the basic disciplines are, the necessity of teaching them, as well as how best to teach them.

ESTABLISH A MENTORING RELATIONSHIP

Mentoring is a partnership between God, other mentors, the Word, the Holy Spirit, and the person being mentored. Paul described the mentoring relationship in 1 Corinthians 3:3: "I planted the seed, Apollos watered, but God made it grow" (NIV).

MODEL A BIBLICAL LIFESTYLE

The closer members' values, character, and lifestyle align with biblical Christian living, the greater their influence on each other and on their community. Leaders, individual members, and the church as a whole increase their disciple-making effectiveness by modeling a biblical lifestyle.

Goals of Disciples Committed to Maturity

When do we know the individual has committed to maturity and the church is effectively practicing the Law of Instruction?

When believers commit to lifelong spiritual growth and development, elevating their whole life—awareness, attitudes, and actions—to a higher spiritual plane.

At Base 2 true disciples reflect the following growth in the following areas:

AWARENESS GOALS

People commit to maturity when their awareness is enlightened and they (1) know that the baptism in the Holy Spirit is for all believers, bringing a supernatural power for life as a witness; (2) know that Christlikeness is the aim of the Christian life; (3) know that loving God is the primary directive of the disciple's life; (4) know that loving God is shown by our love for others; and (5) know the biblical principles and commands that provide guidance in faith and conduct.

ATTITUDE GOALS

People commit to maturity by an *attitude* that (1) desires the baptism in the Holy Spirit, (2) desires a Christlike life, (3) desires to love God fully, (4) is concerned with the spiritual and physical needs of others, and (5) desires to live by biblical principles and commands.

ACTION GOALS

People commit to maturity when they take *action* and (1) enter into a Spirit-filled life by seeking and receiving the baptism in the Holy Spirit, (2) make the principles and commands of the Bible the ruling factor in all decisions, (3) develop a consistent pattern of corporate and personal prayer and worship, (4) respond to the spiritual and physical needs of others, and (5) study the Bible in a regular and systematic manner.

Profile of Disciples Committed to Maturity

Disciples committed to maturity grow. Putting Christ first, they live separated from sin and dedicated to God. They grow in the Word through regular, systematic Scripture study and memorization. With the help of the Holy Spirit, they consistently apply the principles and commands of the Bible to their decision making as well as their whole lives. They maintain a consistent devotional life, growing in faith, character, and intercessory prayer. They enter a Spirit-filled life by being baptized in the Holy Spirit. They attend church regularly, showing Christ's love by identifying with and serving other believers. They identify with Him where they live and work, manifest a heart for witnessing, give a clear testimony, and present the gospel with increasing effectiveness. As disciples they are open and teachable. They are visible followers and learners of Jesus Christ.

Resources

These resources, available from Gospel Publishing House, and activities intentionally focus on helping believers develop the values, character, and lifestyles of true disciples.

ADULT SUNDAY SCHOOL CLASSES

Radiant Life Curriculum for adults and young adults and the Spiritual Discovery Series

NEW BELIEVERS/DISCIPLESHIP CLASSES AND HOME BIBLE STUDIES

Beating Mediocrity, by John Guest (03-1109)
Your New Life in Christ, by Michael Clarensau (02-0766)
Pentecostal Experience: The Writings of Donald Gee, ed. David Womack (02-0454)

1
The Case for Maturity

First Church was a church in crisis. The congregation had recently elected a new pastor who brought change to the stagnant congregation. Now change was coming to the Sunday school department. Polly had been the Sunday school superintendent for years. In fact, she had founded the Sunday school. But the new pastor was asking her to assume a different role. Every member feared that Polly would leave First Church. After all, it was *her* Sunday School! Polly stood before the Sunday school staff to announce her decision. Everyone waited anxiously. Polly declared, "I love this Sunday school. In fact, I founded this Sunday school. I believe in this church, and I believe in this pastor. Greater days are ahead for First Church!" The group sat in stunned silence and then stood as one applauding Polly.

The preceding situation occurs in churches all over America. Unfortunately, the outcome isn't always the same as in First Church. So what was different about First Church? What was different about Polly? Polly was mature. Mature believers seek God's best for themselves, the church, and others. Mature believers make great leaders and wonderful team members!

Maturity Defined

A dictionary definition of *maturity* is "full development." Maturation is further described as "the emergence of personal and behavioral characteristics through growth processes." All living things go through such a process. Just as living things go through the process of physical maturation, all believers should go through a process of spiritual maturation. In spiritual development, maturity is a Christian lifestyle developed by learning the principles of Christ and practicing them through the empowerment of the Holy Spirit. The Bible is addressing maturity when it says Scripture is "profitable for doctrine, for reproof, for correction, for instruction in righteousness: That the man of God may be *perfect, thoroughly furnished unto all good works*" (2 Timothy 3:16,17, KJV, emphasis added).

Note the goal being identified by Paul:

> "That the man of God may be perfect, thoroughly furnished unto all good works." The Greek word behind "perfect" is *artios*,... "fit, complete, sufficient; able to meet all demands." Generally this relates to one's character—who a person is. God's primary goal is that every believer's character be transformed over time into the image of Jesus. The second [part of this goal] is "thoroughly furnished" and comes from the Greek word *exertismenos,* which is related to the same root word as *artios.* It means "completely outfitted, fully furnished, fully equipped, and fully supplied." For what purpose? For "all good works." In this way the believer's conduct is appropriate and active in serving the Lord. God gave the Bible to accomplish two goals: change in character (who I am) and conduct (what I do). If the believer is not becoming more Christlike ... and ... if he is not being equipped for effective service, then Scripture is not fulfilling its purpose in that believer's life.[1]

The goal of every church, Sunday school class, small group, or discipleship program should be to produce maturity in the lives of its members. This is true for every age level and at every stage of spiritual development! To program and plan for maturity, teachers, pastors, and leaders must have a basic understanding of spiritual maturity.

Facts About Spiritual Maturity

MATURITY IS NOT DETERMINED BY AGE

The world equates age with maturity. People automatically assume that the gray-headed senior citizen is mature and the energetic adolescent is immature. Psalm 119:100 indicates a different criteria for maturity in God's kingdom: "I have more understanding than the elders, for I obey your precepts."

The Psalmist indicates that a youth is able to have a greater degree of understanding than elders by meditating on the Word of God and following its instructions. Age does not determine maturity; rather, obedience to the Word determines maturity. It is never too early nor never too late to decide to grow.

MATURITY IS NOT DETERMINED BY EDUCATION

Many believers mistakenly assume that knowledge of the Scriptures, theology, eschatology, or biblical history produces maturity. Being able to list the fruit of the Spirit in no way guarantees their operation. Knowledge of the Ten Commandments does not ensure living by them. Information without application yields no fruit. Maturity occurs where information and application meet. Can a believer with a sixth-grade education be more mature than a Bible college graduate? Yes, by understanding the principles of the Word and applying them to life. Psalm 119:99 says, "I have more insight than all my teachers, for I meditate on your statutes."

The Psalmist had more understanding than those with more education. Why? Meditation on the Word of God and obedience to its principles. In addition to knowledge, spiritual maturity includes a believer's character and conduct.

MATURITY IS A COMMITMENT TO LIFELONG SPIRITUAL GROWTH AND DEVELOPMENT

Maturity requires time, commitment, and effort to grow. Spiritual growth does not automatically follow conversion. Hebrews 5:12,13 illustrates this:

Though by this time you ought to be teachers, you need someone
to teach you the elementary truths of God's word all over again.
You need milk, not solid food! Anyone who lives on milk, being
still an infant, is not acquainted with the teaching about righteousness.

The writer of Hebrews compares these immature people to
babies that have not even matured to solid food. Growing in
God is a decision. A person must have the desire to grow and
be willing to make the necessary effort. Philippians 2:12,13
further illustrates this point: "Continue to work out your salvation with fear and trembling, for it is God who works in you
to will and to act according to his good purpose."

Notice that it says "work out" not "work on" your salvation.
There is nothing you can add to what Christ did for your salvation. In these verses Paul is talking about spiritual growth to
people who are already saved. God has a part in our growth,
but so do we.

"Becoming like Christ is the result of the commitments we
make. We become whatever we are committed to. Without a
commitment to grow, any growth that occurs will be incidental,
rather than intentional."[2]

Spiritual growth that leads to maturity begins with the kind
of commitment described in Romans 6:13: "Offer yourselves to
God, as those who have been brought from death to life; and
offer the parts of your body to him as instruments of righteousness." Spiritual growth does not always come easy. It takes
effort.

MATURITY IS A PROCESS

We live in an age of instant everything. With the advent of credit
cards, we don't have to wait for anything. We can have it all now.
We may end up spending the rest of our lives paying for it, but
it's ours for the charging. Maturity doesn't work that way. In the
Christian life, there's no such thing as quickie quality or micro-
wave maturity. Most of us have a hard time understanding that

God isn't in a hurry. He doesn't rush the development of our Christian life. When we're first saved, it's common to experience a period of rapid growth. God knows we need to develop a strong root system. But that doesn't continue. God also knows that if there's to be healthy development, the pace must be modified.[3]

There are no shortcuts to maturity. Maturity takes time, effort, and determination. Many people search for a quick answer, a key, that will accelerate them through the process of maturity. No such key exists. "Grow in the grace and knowledge of our Lord and Savior Jesus Christ" (2 Peter 3:18).

The process of maturity continues for a lifetime. A Christian should always be growing and learning. James describes the sequence God uses to produce maturity in the lives of His children, saying,

> Consider it pure joy, my brothers, whenever you face trials of many kinds, because you know that the testing of your faith develops perseverance. Perseverance must finish its work so that you may be mature and complete, not lacking anything (James 1:2–4).

Perseverance is a word that many have grown to hate. A dictionary definition reveals why: "to persist in a state, enterprise, or undertaking in spite of counter influences, opposition, or discouragement." Persevering is not fun. However, James indicates it is essential for producing maturity. God uses testing in the process of building our maturity to ensure that our character keeps up with our conduct and our knowledge.

MATURITY TAKES DISCIPLINE

First Timothy 4:7 says: "Train yourself to be godly." The word *training* seldom evokes positive images—basic training, potty training, pet training. Training can be distasteful, boring, frustrating—besides requiring self-discipline.

Consider beginning distance runners. Their training schedule is geared toward running the marathon. The first day calls for a mile. But by the half-mile mark, legs are in knots, stomachs are tightening, and lungs are burning. The mile seems like a marathon. But each day they run a bit farther. They are bothered in the middle of the night by muscle cramps as leg muscles complain at being pushed to new limits. They awaken to sore, stiff muscles, begging for a day off or to just take it easy. But the distance runner stretches those legs and begins to run again, often repeating the familiar mantra: "no pain, no gain." Jose Ortega Y. Gasset said it this way: "Effort is only effort when it begins to hurt." So pushing the limits of the body gains strength and endurance beyond previous limitations. And one day, months later, the body is finally built up to the point where it is able to run a complete marathon.

Paul compares our Christian walk to this distance runner:

> Not that I have already obtained all this, or have already been made perfect, but I press on to take hold of that for which Christ Jesus took hold of me. Brothers, I do not consider myself yet to have taken hold of it. But one thing I do: Forgetting what is behind and straining toward what is ahead, I press on toward the goal to win the prize for which God has called me heavenward in Christ Jesus. All of us who are mature should take such a view of things (Philippians 3:12–15).

To continue to grow in spiritual maturity, we, like the distance runner, often must do what is difficult. It is hard to maintain the daily discipline of Bible study, prayer, and meditation. At times it is difficult to get out of bed on Sunday mornings or rush from work to church on Wednesday evenings. But the Christian who is maturing understands the need for perseverance.

MATURITY IS A GOAL

Maturity is not a destination. There is infinite room for a believer to mature. We will never achieve total Christlikeness until we reach heaven. Paul spoke to the church in Corinth about our final perfection: "Now we see but a poor reflection as in a mirror; then we shall see face to face. Now I know in part; then I shall know fully, even as I am fully known" (1 Corinthians 13:12).

Throughout the life of a believer, maturity must remain the goal. From the general superintendent of the Assemblies of God to the beginning Christian, every believer must continue to mature.

Understanding Discipleship

A mature believer is called a disciple. When every department, Sunday school class, small group, pastor, and leader accepts the goal of producing mature believers, the result is disciples.

In the first century, disciples were individuals who attached themselves to someone else in order to learn from that person. The student was referred to as a disciple. The person they followed was referred to as teacher. The ancient Greek method of discipleship gives further insight into the meaning:

The Greek schoolchildren did not have to sit at desks in classrooms. Instead, they were deposited by their proud parents or long-suffering slaves at a grove where lemons and oranges and olives grew. In the shade of these lovely, aromatic trees stood the teacher, clad in a long white robe and matching beard. Once the pupils (disciples) were assembled, he would start walking among the trees, sharing with them the lesson for the hour. The pupils would follow their teacher as he walked; and no doubt, being kids, they would begin to imitate his every gesture and idiosyncrasy. In time they would learn something despite themselves, and what they learned would show up in conscious and unconscious behaviors. To the Greek mind, discipleship meant following, learning, and imitating. All three concepts are strikingly evident in the impact Christ had on His disciples and are equally powerful in shaping the modern-day disciple.[4]

What, then, is a disciple? Someone who has an ongoing personal relationship with a teacher, whose life is a pattern to be imitated. The habits, speech, personality, behavior, reactions, and attitudes of the disciple are patterned after those of the teacher. Luke describes the relationship: "Everyone who is fully trained will be like his teacher" (Luke 6:40). As a result of this life-oriented following, the student then gladly shares that learning with others.

What is the goal of the church? The goal of the church is to produce disciples of Jesus Christ. As we produce disciples, the exponential effect is amazing! In an effective church, each disciple produces other disciples, who produce other disciples, who produce other disciples. The mature believer, while following the example of Christ, is continually seeking to lead others along the same path.

The disciple is not marked by knowledge, but by obedience. Discipleship is knowing *and* obeying the commands of Jesus. Naturally, a disciple of Jesus Christ develops habits that are in conformity to Jesus' character and will. "Men decide their habits; their habits decide their future."[5] There are many habits to develop; but five primary habits are found in maturing believers.

Five Habits of a Disciple

BIBLE READING

Human opposition has never been able to overcome the power in the Word of God. Disciples understand the power that is available to them as they meditate upon the Scriptures. "Discipleship means continually changing to become more and more like Jesus Christ. That's what our time in Scripture should lead to."[6]

Your strength depends exclusively and entirely upon how much of the Word you get in you. In fact, a recent survey revealed that the more people read their Bible, the happier they become.

The study found that nearly 90 percent of frequent Bible readers say they feel at peace all or most of the time, compared to 58 percent of people who read the Bible less than once a month. Other findings: 92 percent of frequent Bible readers report knowing a clear purpose and meaning in life compared to 69 percent of infrequent readers. Eighty-one percent of frequent readers say they feel content most or all of the time compared to 67 percent of the infrequent Bible readers. Nearly two-thirds (64 percent) of frequent readers say they feel joy all or most of the time—a figure almost twice that of those who read the Bible less than monthly.[7]

The Word will work in your heart and life. Consider these descriptions of the force of the Word:

1. The Word is a devouring flame (Jeremiah 5:14).
2. The Word is like a crushing hammer (Jeremiah 23:29).
3. The Word is like a life-giving force (Ezekiel 37:7).
4. The Word is like a saving power (Romans 1:16).
5. The Word is like a defensive weapon (Ephesians 6:17).
6. The Word is like a probing instrument (Hebrews 4:12).

The Word of God is a quick and powerful, life-giving Word. It is a shield for defense and a sword for attack. Mature believers understand the power they possess when they read the Word of God daily. The Bible says even our prosperity and success depend on the Word! "Do not let this Book of the Law depart from your mouth; meditate on it day and night, so that you may be careful to do everything written in it. Then you will be prosperous and successful" (Joshua 1:8). Disciples are committed to daily time in the Word of God. It is the handbook for Christian discipleship.

PRAYER

A consistent prayer life is not an option for a disciple. To become like the Master, you must spend regular time with Him.

Prayer is our means of communication with our Heavenly Father. Prayer is not primarily about learning or having an emotional experience. Prayer is primarily an act of love. When we pray, in addition to expressing our needs, we communicate our love to our Heavenly Father. Then, in the quietness of our devotional time, He speaks words of hope, encouragement, strength, courage, and healing to our spirits.

There is power in prayer. Jesus spoke of the power of prayer: "If you remain in me and my words remain in you, ask whatever you wish, and it will be given you. This is to my Father's glory, that you bear much fruit, showing yourselves to be my disciples" (John 15:7,8).

Nehemiah is a great example of a man who made prayer his first priority. When he heard that Jerusalem's walls were still in disrepair and ruin, he sought the Lord for days with weeping and fasting (see Nehemiah 1:2–4). Prayer came first. The actual rebuilding of the walls came later. Prayer was the priority that brought the breakthrough of God's purposes in the matter.

Prayer is, first of all, God's agency to bring us to himself. It lies at the heart of our relatedness to God. In the act of praying, we confront God for who He is. We begin to realize our seeking is often more important to God than our having. Indeed, we need prayer more than God needs prayer.

It is, therefore, not surprising that individuals of continued and extended prayer often become persons with great zeal and passion for God, enthusiastic disciples! If our hearts are to stay uncluttered from the loves, desires, and distractions of our world, they must be continually drawn to God and exercised in prayer. He wants us, and He wants to fill our hearts with His heart. That is His priority. Prayer is God's agency by which it happens.

Prayer also extends God's agenda in the world. Nehemiah's first response on hearing bad news was not to take matters into his own hands. Instead, he became a partner with God to advance a divine agenda. This is called "praying in the will of

God." Prayer becomes a priority because it embraces God's will to intervene in the lives of people, churches, and nations. Prayer is not twisting the arm of a reluctant God; it is embracing the heart of a willing God.

The disciple understands that prayer is the primary method for communication with the Master. The disciple sets a daily prayer time as part of his or her personal schedule. Prayer is essential to the disciple's continued growth.

ATTENDANCE

A disciple understands the importance of attending church regularly. Hebrews 10:25 gives the biblical mandate for this habit: "Let us not give up meeting together, as some are in the habit of doing, but let us encourage one another—and all the more as you see the Day approaching."

Attending church does not automatically create a Christian. However, attending church helps the disciple develop a consistent life in accordance with God's standards. The disciple attends church for three primary reasons.

1. **Ensure continual growth.** A disciple is committed to a lifetime of growth. How do children grow? Children grow physically as they are fed food. They grow intellectually as they are taught. They grow spiritually in direct proportion to the amount and quality of godly instruction they receive. How do disciples ensure continual growth? They grow by seeking new information, deeper truths, and freshly revealed biblical principles. It is possible to grow spiritually without attending church, but not probable.

2. **Ministry to others.** There are many avenues for ministry. One of the primary places to minister is in church. Disciples serve in key leadership positions in the local church as Sunday school teachers, board members, ushers, greeters, nursery workers, etc. Discipleship is most effective when disciples are creating disciples! Where does this often occur? At church. The mature believer attends church

not only to receive spiritual direction, but to lead others
into maturity.
3. **Example to others.** The disciple attends church regularly because it is the right thing to do. Leaders are continually watched by others. Leaders model the behavior they
want others to follow. At one church, members are asked,
"If everyone attended church like you attend, what kind of
church would this be?" Mature believers model maturity.

TITHING

What is tithing? The word *tithe* means "tenth." Tithing is
returning to God the 10 percent of your total income which He
personally has designated for himself.

A disciple is marked by obedience in giving to God. Many
believers are not tithers; in addition, preachers are reluctant to
confront their congregations about this. They fear alienating
them or appearing greedy. But tithing is God's command to the
believer: "A tithe of everything from the land, whether grain
from the soil or fruit from the trees, belongs to the Lord; it is
holy to the LORD" (Leviticus 27:30).

Some people feel that these Scripture passages applied to the
Old Testament Israelites only. However, I think a little further
study proves otherwise. First, Abraham gave tithe *before* the
Law was given to Moses. Second, Jesus recognized it as a worth-
while practice even among the unworthy Pharisees (see Matthew
23:23). Third, if it was meant for the seed of Abraham, that includes those in Christ. "If you belong to Christ, then you are
Abraham's seed, and heirs according to the promise" (Galatians
3:29). Fourth, there is no Scripture passage that refutes tithing
to render it an obsolete practice.[8]

Everything we have was given to us by God. In fact, God
owns all the money! "'The silver is mine and the gold is mine,'
declares the Lord Almighty" (Haggai 2:8).

The disciple not only gives, but enjoys giving to God and His
church. A consistent habit of giving indicates the priority that

following the Master has in one's life. "The purpose of tithing is to teach you always to put God first in your lives" (Deuteronomy 14:23, *The Living Bible*). Tithing is a distinguishing trait of discipleship.

When we give to God, we begin a cycle of blessing that is perpetual. The seeds we plant in God's kingdom produce a harvest in our own lives. According to Jesus' own words, an individual who is unwilling to become a tither and a giver simply cannot be a disciple. "Any of you who does not give up everything he has cannot be my disciple" (Luke 14:33).

WITNESSING

Effective disciples share what they have found. Witnessing is a command of Jesus to His disciples: "Therefore go and make disciples of all nations, baptizing them in the name of the Father and of the Son and of the Holy Spirit, and teaching them to obey everything I have commanded you. And surely I am with you always, to the very end of the age" (Matthew 28:19,20).

> The "going" for a considerable number of Christians will entail crossing an ocean, but for those who honestly believe that this is not what the Master wants for them, the command is no less crucial. How about traveling across town to another ethnic group in the same city, or across the street to a neighborhood family, or even across the office to a colleague? There is always somewhere to go, and that means crossing some kind of barrier—whether geographical, political, sociological, or just plain psychological. It should be apparent to all disciples in any era that the discipling of nations does not happen when the disciples who know don't go.[9]

It is a rare person who comes to the saving knowledge of Jesus without a messenger, someone to carry the divine invitation of the gospel. Excited about personal transformation, a disciple cannot wait to see the same transformation occur in others! A person who discovered the fountain of youth would share it with the world. Why? Because it would change the way people live. A person who discovered a safe, effective, easy way to lose excess weight would share it with the world. (Undoubtedly, he would make millions!) Why? It would change people's lives. Our knowledge of the saving grace of Jesus Christ will change people's lives in an even greater way!

The simple message of the gospel changes lives and transforms character. "If you own a Bible, then you have been entrusted with a lifetime supply of seeds. Don't underestimate your capacity to plant them in the lives of your non-Christian friends!"[10] Disciples are continually looking for opportunities to introduce others to their Teacher. Ask yourself this question: Who are the people around me whose lives are being so influenced by me that they too are becoming disciples?

Immaturity

If prayer, Bible reading, tithing, and witnessing are marks of maturity in the lives of believers, what are the characteristics of immaturity? One of the most notable examples of immaturity in the Bible is Samson. God gifted Samson with great strength; He anointed him as a deliverer for his people. Samson's mighty exploits thrill Sunday school classes, inspiring young boys to flex their muscles and slay enemies! But Samson, in spite of God's power, lost it all. If you observe the life of Samson, you will see the peril of living a less-than-committed lifestyle. When you do not live a totally dedicated life, every day, in every way, you run the risk of following Samson's path. Samson lived by his feelings rather than by his commitments.

Are you an immature believer? Truthfully answer these 10 questions:

1. Do I lose my temper frequently?
2. Do I repeatedly make the same mistakes?
3. Do I make decisions against the counsel of my spiritual authorities?

4. Do I have unresolved conflicts with other people?
5. Am I less than faithful in tithing to my local church?
6. Do I often miss my prayer and Bible study time due to busyness or fatigue?
7. Do I attend church at my convenience, often missing services?
8. Do I make promises to God that I am unable to keep?
9. Are there times when others would characterize me as out of control?
10. Do I harbor grudges against those who have wronged me?

If you answered yes to any of the above questions, you have identified an area of immaturity in your life. If you answered several of the questions yes, you have cause for great concern.

Characteristics of Immaturity

As has been noted, the Old Testament story of Samson reveals that immaturity, among other things, led to Samson's downfall. His immaturity manifested itself in the following ways.

REBELLIOUS LIFESTYLE

Samson yielded to the lust of the flesh. In three different chapters, he is enamored of three different women. He keeps running in and out of relationships. In Judges 14:1,2 we read, "Samson went down to Timnah and saw there a young Philistine woman. When he returned, he said to his father and mother, 'I have seen a Philistine woman in Timnah; now get her for me as my wife.'"

In essence, Samson said, "She pleases me, she looks good to me." *Immature people make decisions based on pleasure instead of principle.* When we start to live our lives out of caprice rather than conviction, we are headed for trouble. Samson made a vow not to marry an unbeliever. God warned Samson. His parents warned him. But Samson ignored his vow, his parents, and his

God, and married her. Samson threw away his life's plan for a season of pleasure.

Many people make promises to God. In a teary-eyed moment of surrender, they pledge to again honor their marriage vows. Teenagers pledge to remain pure until marriage. The recovering alcoholic pledges to never drink again. The wavering college student vows to find the right kind of friend. The busy housewife decides to set aside a time every day for prayer, Bible reading, and meditation. It is a good thing when believers pledge to honor God in their habits. The immature will walk away from commitment in favor of immediate gratification.

Many people come to the altar each Sunday to confess to the same sin. At the close of the service, they once again walk down the aisle and vow to God that it will never happen again. Yet, that week, they again break their pledge. Is their repentance insincere? No. They are immature. The Holy Spirit's power can help a believer discipline desires. The once-impulsive Peter wrote of the Holy Spirit's role in Christian growth:

> Therefore, since Christ suffered in his body, arm yourselves also with the same attitude, because he who has suffered in his body is done with sin. As a result, he does not live the rest of his earthly life for evil human desires, but rather for the will of God. For you have spent enough time in the past doing what pagans choose to do—living in debauchery, lust, drunkenness, orgies, carousing and detestable idolatry.... The end of all things is near. Therefore be clear minded and self-controlled so that you can pray (1 Peter 4:1–3,7).

The immature believer has not yet learned to control desires in accordance with the Word of God. Immaturity expresses itself as rebellion.

RESENTFUL

People will hurt you, let you down, and break their promises. It is easy to become resentful. Samson lived in a constant state of anger. He reacted violently to everything. His primary motivation in life was to get even. One time he killed 30 men, just to get even on a bet! Judges 15 gives a descriptive picture of Samson's simmering resentment:

> Later on, at the time of wheat harvest, Samson took a young goat and went to visit his wife. He said, "I'm going to my wife's room." But her father would not let him go in. "I was so sure you thoroughly hated her," he said, "that I gave her to your friend. Isn't her younger sister more attractive? Take her instead." Samson said to them, *"This time I have a right to get even with the Philistines; I will really harm them."* So he went out and caught three hundred foxes and tied them tail to tail in pairs. He then fastened a torch to every pair of tails, lit the torches and let the foxes loose in the standing grain of the Philistines. He burned up the shocks and standing grain, together with the vineyards and olive groves. When the Philistines asked, "Who did this?" they were told, "Samson, the Timnite's son-in-law, because his wife was given to his friend." So the Philistines went up and burned her and her father to death. Samson said to them, *"Since you've acted like this, I won't stop until I get my revenge on you."* He attacked them viciously and slaughtered many of them. Then he went down and stayed in a cave in the rock of Etam. The Philistines went up and camped in Judah, spreading out near Lehi. The men of Judah asked, "Why have you come to fight us?" "We have come to take Samson prisoner," they answered, "to do to him as he did to us." Then three thousand men from Judah went down to the cave in the rock of Etam and said to Samson, "Don't you realize that the Philistines are rulers over us? What have you done to us?" He answered, *"I merely did to them what they did to me"* (Judges 15:1–11, emphasis added).

Samson said, "I'm going to get even." He said it three times in one chapter! Samson's excuse was that they hurt him first. He was reacting in anger instead of acting in obedience.

Immature people react with resentment, anger, and violent outbursts of temper. When people lose control, they have marked themselves as immature! Proverbs 29:11 says: "A fool gives full vent to his anger, but a wise man keeps himself under control." Resentment is self-defeating. Job 5:2 says, "Resent-ment kills a fool." You cannot hold on to grudges and follow the will of God.

People leave churches, friendships, and relationships over the smallest things. A longtime member may leave the church because no one called him last Sunday when he was sick. A student may leave your class after 10 years because of not being chosen for a position. Adult children refuse to see their siblings because they said the wrong thing at the dinner table last Thanksgiving. Immature people nurse their resentments until they become grudges. They feed their grudges until they become offenses. They carry their offenses until they dictate behavior. People full of the Holy Spirit must learn to restrain their reactions.

RECKLESS

Immature people are reckless. *They are careless with their money, words, time, commitments, and affections.*

Samson continually compromised his commitment based on caprice. He toyed with temptation. He was reckless once too often and Delilah cut his hair, the source of his strength. After Delilah cut his hair and he woke up, he said: "I will go out as at other times before, and shake myself. And he wist not that the LORD was departed from him" (Judges 16:20, KJV).

Samson walked close to the edge. He knew the power of God and the strength he possessed, but he was reckless. He took chances. With each chance he took, he became further emboldened, more reckless. Finally, the last time, he went too far.

People do not fall off the cliff of character overnight. It starts with small steps in that direction. They know the fire of the Spirit; God has touched them. But they cool off. Immature people become reckless with the precious gifts of God. They trade their commitment for convenience, God's power for personality, and anointing for approval. Eventually they reach the place where purity is practiced on a part-time basis. They become reckless with their convictions and even their salvation.

Denying Yourself

If, unlike Samson, we are going to discipline our desires, restrain our reactions, and keep our commitments, we must learn the proper method. It can be summed up in two words: *deny self*. Paul said, "I die every day" (1 Corinthians 15:31). Did Paul physically die every day? Of course not. Paul learned that to grow and mature and become more like Jesus, he had to die to himself every day. What does it mean to die to self? These 10 statements offer some perspective:

1. When you can watch your peers and those close to you prosper and succeed without feeling jealous, but rather rejoice, then you can know the meaning of dying to self.
2. When you can watch others—without being envious— attain goals you fail to reach and receive rewards and recognition you would like to have, that's dying to self.
3. When you can watch other people's needs being met abundantly when your needs are far greater, and you don't question God or fail to be grateful for what you have, that's denying self.
4. When you don't seek praise or compliments or approval, and when you can live without frequent recognition and applause, that's denying self.
5. When you can accept criticism willingly and learn from it with a teachable attitude, and when you allow others to do a job that you know you are better trained to do, that's denying self.
6. When you submit to an authority over you in deference to God even though you don't agree or understand, that's denying self.
7. When you can be content with less than the best of circumstances without griping or complaining, that's denying self.

8. When you can accept interruptions that God places in your schedule and patiently bear with irritations, that's denying self.
9. When you are content to let God settle the score and content to wait for your reward in heaven, that's denying self.
10. When you have the attitude of Jesus, that's denying self.

2
Characteristics
of Maturity

If a mature believer is a disciple, then discipleship is the process by which additional mature believers are produced. This is the exciting aspect of maturity! Disciples, when properly equipped, will function in the primary role of a disciple: producing other disciples. The benefits of this "multiplication ministry" are enormous. How many pastors have felt overwhelmed at the prospect of leading hundreds of church members into maturity? Sunday school teachers are often overwhelmed at leading a large class into life as disciples. But multiplication ministry expands the teacher's influence in a rapid fashion. Jesus understood the value of multiplication. Hundreds and thousands of people followed Jesus; they all longed to spend daily time with him. He could have spent every day preaching to a crowd of thousands. Yet He chose the Twelve to be His disciples. From the throngs of people, He selected 12 men of varying backgrounds and personalities to walk by His side. Why? Jesus understood the limitations of His human form. As a man, He could be in only one place at a time, ministering to one group of people. He could not carry out the work of spreading the gospel by himself. Even Jesus recognized the power of reproducing himself in others. So He chose to spend large amounts of time with the Twelve, teaching them, leading them, and demonstrating ministry to them. In turn, the Twelve were then given the task of going and producing more disciples. They would communicate to their followers everything they had learned from the Master. This multiplication continued throughout the New Testament and even to today.

So what is your job as a disciple? Your job is to teach others what you have learned, to create additional disciples. The same habits that you exhibit will be exhibited in the lives of your disciples. The primary habits of prayer, Bible reading, church attendance, tithing, and witnessing should be reproduced in your disciples.

Discipleship in the local church can take place in many different forms. Sunday school is the primary means of discipleship in many churches. Discipleship groups can also be created to work through a specified course of study in a specified time. Individuals can disciple others in a one-on-one relationship. New converts can be discipled in a class created to introduce them to the basic doctrines of the church. Children, youth, adults, all segments of the church, can become involved in the process of discipleship. There is no limit to the different programs and methods that can be utilized to create disciples.

Many people are reluctant to become involved in discipleship because they don't understand its purpose. Some confuse discipleship with mentoring, some with evangelism. All three ministries are important to the body of Christ. However, to function in discipleship, one must understand the differences. The following chart will help clarify different aspects of each ministry:

	EVANGELISM	DISCIPLESHIP	MENTORING
Is it scriptural?	Taught and modeled in Scripture	Taught and modeled in Scripture	Modeled in Scripture
Models in Scripture	Paul	Timothy	Barnabas

	EVANGELISM	DISCIPLESHIP	MENTORING
How great is the need?	Desperate	Desperate	Desperate
Primary basis of interchange	Content	Content	Relationship
Type of role	Convincing nonbelievers and defending the faith, presenting the Good News	Teaching new believers spiritual truths	Caring for and helping a person in all aspects of life
Whose agenda?	Evangelist's agenda (the gospel)	Discipler's agenda (spiritual guidelines)	Protégé's agenda (goals/problems)
Training required	Person equipped as evangelist	Academic knowledge and personal mastery of spiritual disciplines	Practical life experience relevant to protégé
Time frame	Less than one hour (typically)	Prescribed course of study	Lifelong as needed
Focus of time together	Presenting the salvation opportunity	Teaching the spiritual disciplines	Supporting in all areas of life
Sequence in growth process	Must come first	Can begin at any time	Begin after salvation
Importance of personal chemistry	Respect required	Respect required	Respect and personal chemistry both required
Approximate numbers involved	Possibly thousands evangelized over a lifetime	Possibly hundreds discipled over a lifetime	Small numbers mentored in a lifetime
Modern role parallels	Brilliant, articulate, evangelists/ apologists	Disciplined, mature teacher	Loving aunt, uncle, or close friend

	EVANGELISM	DISCIPLESHIP	MENTORING
Essential message	Repent, you must be saved! The kingdom of God is at hand.	To mature spiritually, here is what you need to know, do, or become.	How can I help you get where you are going?
Result of relationship	Salvation or rejection	Reproducing disciples	Lifelong friendship
Who should be involved?	All unbelievers	All believers	Anyone desiring the relationship[11]

It is our task to create discipleship opportunities for every believer at every stage of spiritual development. For discipleship to operate correctly in the local church setting, several building blocks must be in place.

Building Block #1: Accountability

For discipleship to occur, there must be an atmosphere of accountability established. Accountability is a term that has been much abused in recent years. Accountability is not the teacher directing every detail of the disciple's life. Instead, accountability is offered to the teacher by the disciple. Accountability is an upward word: subordinate to superior. For accountability to function properly, it must be offered, never demanded.

The marriage relationship is a perfect example of accountability. Consider the following scenario where accountability is neglected:

Mary is sitting at the kitchen table, preparing her Sunday school lesson for the next morning. Her husband, David, walks past her without saying a word, opens the garage, and takes off in his car. He goes to the service station and gets the oil changed. He returns an hour later to an angry wife, demanding to know where he went.

What has happened? No accountability was offered. Instead, an explanation was demanded. The result is tension.

Now consider the same scenario with an attitude of accountability:

Mary is sitting at the kitchen table, preparing her Sunday school lesson. Her husband, David, walks into the room and says, "Honey, I'm going to get the oil changed in the car. I'll be back in about an hour. Do you need anything while I'm out?" She says, "No, thanks. I'll see you later." David goes to the garage, and drives off. He has the oil changed and returns in an hour to a happy home.

What has happened? David offered accountability to his wife. The result is an atmosphere of mutual agreement.

Accountability is essential in a church. It offers the teacher or discipler the opportunity to mold and shape the life of the student, beyond just transmitting information. How does accountability function in the church?

1. The Sunday school teacher informs the superintendent that he is going to be running late the next 3 weeks due to his work situation. Instead of arriving at 9:30 A.M., 30 minutes before the start of class, he will arrive at 10 A.M.
2. The class member calls the teacher to let her know he is having difficulty completing that week's assignment. His children have been sick, and he has had to care for them instead of studying.
3. The class secretary lets the teacher know that she will be on vacation and will miss the next two Sunday mornings.
4. The staff member informs the pastor that her husband has the flu and won't be in church this morning.

In each of the above, accountability has been offered. Each situation could have resulted in tension. However, because someone took the initiative to offer accountability, everyone works together for the common good. The result of each situation?

1. Instead of wondering why her star teacher is suddenly showing up barely on time, the superintendent covers for

him prior to class time. She has a volunteer arrange the room and greet the class members as they arrive. When the teacher's work situation stabilizes, he resumes his regular routine of arriving at 9:30. He has a new appreciation for his superintendent.

2. Instead of dismissing the student as lazy and lacking motivation, the teacher has extra patience with the student. As a parent, she understands the difficulty of sick children. In addition, she enlists class members to help prepare a meal for the struggling family. The kids get better, and the class member catches up on his assignments, grateful for the assistance of his class.

3. Instead of being angry with the class secretary for her unexplained absences, the teacher arranges for a substitute for the next two Sundays. The secretary returns from her vacation refreshed and ready to serve.

4. Instead of wondering, the pastor knows why the staff member's husband is absent. He even prays for him in the morning service. He is affirmed by his prayers, and is back the next Sunday.

Accountability should be offered on a continuing basis. One pastoral staff member writes,

Several times each year I ask my pastor: Is there anything I am doing or not doing that you need me to change? Is there any way I could be serving you better? This gives the pastor the chance to evaluate me on an ongoing basis. The associate must offer accountability, and the senior pastor, in return, must be willing to confront the associate when correction is needed. This ensures minor issues never become major problems.[12]

Accountability functions in both group and individual settings. A Sunday school teacher offers his accountability to the superintendent and to the pastor. This helps create an atmosphere of trust and teamwork. A small group can create an atmosphere of mutual accountability. Each member of one men's discipleship group fills out a form every week answering the following questions:

1. Did you complete the assignments?
2. This week did you
   A. do anything you weren't supposed to do?
   B. go anywhere you weren't supposed to go?
   C. see anything you weren't supposed to see?
   D. say anything you weren't supposed to say?
3. Did you tell the truth on all of the previous questions?

By answering these tough questions, the men have formed an accountability structure. Many times an atmosphere of accountability serves as a deterrent to sin. When you know someone is going to ask you about your standards this week, you have additional incentive to do what is right.

Building Block #2: Loyalty

The second building block of discipleship is loyalty. A dictionary definition of loyalty is "the quality or state of being loyal." To be loyal means to be "unswerving in allegiance." Loyalty is an essential component in effective relationships. The disciple must be loyal to the leader, and the leader must be loyal to the students.

The quality of loyalty also helps ensure that personal kingdom building does not occur. One of the most harmful things that can occur in a church or department is a leader seeking to establish a personal kingdom, or a "church within the church." This individual seeks to establish a personal agenda, separate from the vision of the church. A biblical example of a personal agenda is found in the person of Absalom.

In the course of time, Absalom provided himself with a chariot and horses and with fifty men to run ahead of him. He would get up early and stand by the side of the road leading to the city gate. Whenever anyone came with a complaint to be placed before the king for a decision, Absalom would call out to him, "What town are you from?" He would answer, "Your servant is from one of the tribes of Israel." Then Absalom would say to him, "Look, your claims are valid and proper, but there is no representative of the king to hear you." And Absalom would add, "If only I were appointed judge in the land! Then everyone who has a complaint or case could come to me and I would see that he gets justice." Also, whenever anyone approached him to bow down before him, Absalom would reach out his hand, take hold of him and kiss him. Absalom behaved in this way toward all the Israelites who came to the king asking for justice, and so he stole the hearts of the men of Israel (2 Samuel 15:1–6).

Absalom sought to undermine the king, his own father, David. The Absalom spirit is subtle and manipulative. It is the opposite of loyalty. The Absalom spirit says, "He doesn't care about your needs, but I care about you." "I know your hurts and will help you, even if no one else will." There are two principles to help you avoid the Absalom spirit.

DEFLECT PRAISE

People will often unwittingly pit their teacher against the pastor or their teacher against another teacher. One way this occurs is through flattery. People love to cheer for the underdog. It is popular to champion the cause of the lesser individual. How does it happen in a church? A class member will approach a teacher and say, "That was a great lesson! I got more out of this than I learned from the sermon." What is he saying? In a subtle, perhaps unknowing way, he is creating tension between the teacher and the pastor. It is difficult to know how to respond to these kinds of comments. An effective way to insulate yourself against an Absalom spirit is to deflect praise. The teacher who has learned how to deflect praise will answer, "Thank you, I am blessed with a wonderful pastor who has taught me a lot." Or "Thank you, I am glad the lesson ministered to you, but I have to tell you: Pastor's sermon really ministered to me."

This technique accomplishes three things. First, it reminds the giver of the praise that you are a loyal team member. Second, it protects you as recipient of the praise from developing a big ego. Third, it creates a team spirit when you acknowledge your efforts are part of a bigger picture.

The pastor or leader uses the same technique to protect himself from improper attitudes. "Leaders we admire do not place themselves at the center; they place others there. They do not seek the attention of people; they give it to others. They do not focus on satisfying their own aims and desires."[13]

Pastors who have learned how to deflect praise will always share their successes with their subordinates. They will often reply to a compliment with, "Thank you. I couldn't do it without a wonderful team of volunteers who work long and hard!" or "Thank you. God has blessed us with a wonderful team!" Leaders who respond in this way affirm their team members and inspire loyalty in those who serve them.

Loyalty is not something a leader can demand. It is something that people choose to give a leader who has earned it. You can inspire loyalty in your disciples!

MINISTER IN JESUS' NAME AND THE PASTOR'S NAME

The second way to avoid an Absalom spirit is to minister in the name of Jesus and your pastor. How do you do this? When you visit class members in the hospital, tell them, "I love you and was worried about you. Pastor Jones is praying for you today as well." This demonstrates to the patient that you care and the pastor cares as well. The opposite approach would say, "Pastor was too busy to visit you today, but I took off work because I care about you." This disloyal approach creates tension in the team and destroys unity. In the same manner, when doing visitation, the pastor says, "I'm praying for you today. I know your teacher and class are praying as well." The patient understands that the team is concerned.

Loyalty allows the teacher and students to operate in an atmosphere of unity. This is vital for discipleship. It is in such an atmosphere that positive, transparent interaction can occur. Without loyalty, the process disintegrates.

Building Block #3: Credibility

To disciple others, you must be a credible leader. The root of credibility is *credo,* meaning "I trust or believe." People are unwilling to follow someone they do not believe. Every teacher, department head, superintendent, and worker has to establish personal credibility. "Without a foundation of personal credibility, leaders can have no hope of enlisting others in a common vision."[14] "The credibility of leadership is what determines whether people will want to give a little more of their time, talent, energy, experience, intelligence, creativity, and support."[15]

In their book *Credibility*, James Kouzes and Barry Pozner list the six disciplines of credibility:

1. **Discovering yourself.** To be credible as a leader, you must first clarify your own values, the standards you choose to live by. To be a credible leader, you must have character, whose essential ingredients are credo, competence, and confidence.
2. **Appreciating constituents.** To be a leader, you must also develop a deep understanding of the collective values and desires of your constituents. Leadership is a relationship, and strong relationships are built on mutual understanding.
3. **Affirming shared values.** Credible leaders honor the diversity of their many constituencies. They also find a common ground for agreement.
4. **Developing capacity.** It is essential for leaders to develop continuously the capacity of their members to keep their commitments. You must educate, educate, educate.
5. **Serving a purpose.** Credible leaders know that it is their visible actions that demonstrate their true commitment.
6. **Sustaining hope.** Credible leaders keep hope alive.

These principles are important in the life of any leader.

Credibility is people believing that what you say is something they can depend upon, something they can immediately believe. Credibility is the consistency between your words and your actions. The teacher who teaches on love must exemplify love. A series on the fruit of the Spirit is quickly undercut by the opposite actions of the teacher, wherever they might occur. People will not allow themselves to be discipled by someone who is not credible.

Building Block #4: Compatibility

The fourth building block of discipleship is compatibility. It is almost impossible to disciple someone if you cannot relate to each other as friends (see John 15:15). For discipleship to function, the teacher and disciple must share common ground. Compatibility is not always automatic. Many times you have to work at getting along with another individual. Several components of compatibility can assist in establishing common ground:

THE MCDONALD HAT THEORY

If you want to work at McDonald's, you have to wear the hat. It does not matter whether you like the hat. It is part of the deal. If you are unwilling to wear the hat, find somewhere else to work. Working in a church has similarities. Many people want to teach a class but don't want the other responsibilities: Every teacher must be committed to thorough preparation, praying for their students, evaluating the needs of their class, calling absentees, caring for the sick, and visitor follow-up. Every teacher has to accept the challenge of producing growth and maturity in the lives of their students. If you do not want the responsibilities, don't teach the class.

THREE CIRCLES OF INTEREST

Every church, every class, has individuals with different interests. Often conflicts arise when we don't understand others' frames of reference. People fall primarily into one of three: corporate, cause, and community. This grid will help you to understand the differences among them.

We need all three types of people in our groups. Understanding the different perspectives of each type will help you to utilize every type of individual in your church or class. Individuals in the corporate circle make excellent Sunday school superintendents, deacons, and building committee members. People in the cause circle are proficient at rallying people around a common need. They are excellent at organizing protests and petitions, distributing voter information guides, and putting together benevolence projects. The individuals in the community circle put together potlucks, are gifted in pastoral care, and make excellent greeters and class secretaries. They love to call people on the phone. They are people persons.

We can learn to get along with others when we understand their strengths and weaknesses. Compatibility occurs when class members are operating in the realm of their gifts and affirming their need for the other gifts.

	COMMUNITY	CAUSE	CORPORATE
Scripture Passage	Acts 2:42	Matthew 16:18	1 Corinthians 14:40
Metaphor	Family	Army	Business
Values	Love	Winning War	Effectiveness and efficiency
Roles	Family: parents, siblings	Military: General, etc.	Employee: CEO, etc.
Key Person	Weakest person	Most committed	Most productive
How to Enter	Born or adopted	Joined or drafted	Hired
How to Exit	You don't	Killed	Fired or quit
Payback	Relationships love and security	Glory, medals	Cash, promotion, stability[16]

CONFLICT RESOLUTION

Every class, every leader, and every disciple will inevitably face conflicts. How these conflicts are handled dramatically affects the organization. Contrary to the belief of many, all conflict is not bad. Conflict in the church is not always a sign of ill health. In fact, conflict produces a great deal of good:

- Issues are fully explored.
- Better decisions are made.
- People are more committed to decisions after discussion.

When conflict is addressed in an atmosphere of cooperation, relationships are strengthened.

AFFIRMING SHARED VALUES

One of the greatest ways to establish compatibility is to affirm the values everyone shares. Shared values are the ground of productive and genuine relationships.

We share some precious common values with those we disciple. We believe Jesus came to this earth as the Son of God, born of a virgin. We believe that He died on a cross for our sins and rose again that we may live forever with Him. We believe that He sent His Holy Spirit to give us comfort and power. Affirming this common ground builds unity. We can tolerate many differences because we serve a great and mighty God.

3
Committing to a Life of Maturity

The mature believer will develop and maintain a daily habit of personal devotion. Daily time in prayer and Bible study is essential to maturity. Our regular time of communion with God allows us to build and strengthen our relationship with Jesus Christ. This habit is a vital key in the life of a believer.

You can teach individuals many great truths from the Word of God. They can attend every service, Sunday school class, and small group meeting. But unless they develop a personal commitment to continued growth, they will not grow. Our relationship with Jesus must move from the corporate setting to a personal one. Corporate growth, although essential, will not lead to individual growth without daily devotion.

In the New Testament, James instructs believers in the importance of continued devotions:

Get rid of all moral filth and the evil that is so prevalent and humbly accept the word planted in you, which can save you. Do not merely listen to the word, and so deceive yourselves. Do what it says. Anyone who listens to the word but does not do what it says is like a man who looks at his face in a mirror and, after looking at himself, goes away and immediately forgets what he looks like. But the man who looks intently into the perfect law that gives freedom, and continues to do this, not forgetting what he has heard, but doing it—he will be blessed in what he does (James 1:21–25).

Verse 25 in the *Jerusalem Bible* reads: "The man who looks steadily at the perfect law of freedom and makes that his *habit*" (emphasis added). James is reminding the New Testament Christians that they must make time in God's Word a habit. Every Christian should have a daily quiet time: a daily time set aside to be alone with God to get to know Him through the Bible and prayer. Saddleback Community Church, in their class "Discovering Spiritual Maturity," teaches each member about having such a routine.

The Priority of a Daily Quiet Time

There are five reasons your time alone with God should be the top priority in your schedule.

WE WERE CREATED FOR COMMUNION WITH GOD

No other part of creation has the privilege of fellowship, dialogue, and communication with the Creator. This is why God created us! From Genesis 1 to the last chapter of the Book of Revelation, God speaks of His desire for fellowship with humanity. God says, "Look! I have been standing at the door and I am constantly knocking. If anyone hears me calling him and opens the door, I will come in and fellowship with him and he with me" (Revelation 3:20, *The Living Bible*).

JESUS DREW STRENGTH FROM HIS DAILY QUIET TIME

The Gospels illustrate the importance that Jesus placed on personal prayer. On many occasions Jesus would separate himself from His disciples, the crowds, and the distractions of the day in order to pray. Consider the following examples:

"And in the morning, rising up a great while before day, he went out, and departed into a solitary place, and there prayed" (Mark 1:35, KJV).

"Jesus went out as usual to the Mount of Olives, and his disciples followed him. On reaching the place, he said to them, 'Pray that you will not fall into temptation.' He withdrew about a stone's throw beyond them, knelt down and prayed" (Luke 22:39–41).

"Yet the news about him spread all the more, so that crowds of people came to hear him and to be healed of their sicknesses. But Jesus often withdrew to lonely places and prayed" (Luke 5:15,16).

Notice the words the authors used to describe Jesus' routine of prayer. "Jesus went out *as usual.*" "*Jesus often* withdrew to lonely places and prayed." The disciples were accustomed to seeing Jesus leave for extended periods of time in order to talk with the Heavenly Father. If Jesus, the Son of God, found His source of strength in prayer, we can also find strength for daily living in our quiet time.

JESUS SACRIFICED HIS LIFE TO ALLOW US TO HAVE A PERSONAL RELATIONSHIP WITH THE HEAVENLY FATHER

Human fellowship with God was broken by sin in the Garden of Eden. Jesus died to restore that fellowship. His death on Calvary allows every believer to experience an intimate relationship with the Father. Paul speaks of this relationship in his letter to the Corinthians, saying: "God will surely do this for you, for he always does just what he says, and he is the one who invited you into this wonderful friendship with his Son, even Christ our Lord" (1 Corinthians 1:9, *The Living Bible*). God invites us to join Him in a wonderful, personal friendship.

YOU CANNOT BE A MATURE CHRISTIAN WITHOUT A REGULAR QUIET TIME

To maintain a healthy growing Christian life, you must have a regular quiet time. The Bible is clear and specific regarding the importance of our communion with God.

"Jesus answered, 'It is written: Man does not live on bread

alone, but on every word that comes from the mouth of God' " (Matthew 4:4).

"I have not departed from the commands of his lips; I have treasured the words of his mouth more than my daily bread" (Job 23:12).

"How can a young man keep his way pure? By living according to your word. I seek you with all my heart; do not let me stray from your commands. I have hidden your word in my heart that I might not sin against you" (Psalm 119:9–11).

A daily quiet time is essential for every Christian!

GREAT MEN OF GOD HAVE MODELED THE HABIT OF A DAILY QUIET TIME

Great men in the Bible modeled the need for a daily quiet time. Men like Abraham, Moses, David, Daniel, and Paul all had an intimate relationship with God. Daniel's personal relationship with God and daily habit of prayer was well known. In fact, it was known even to his enemies.

> Finally these men said, "We will never find any basis for charges against this man Daniel unless it has something to do with the law of his God."
>
> So the administrators and the satraps went as a group to the king and said: "O King Darius, live forever! The royal administrators, prefects, satraps, advisers and governors have all agreed that the king should issue an edict and enforce the decree that anyone who prays to any god or man during the next thirty days, except to you, O king, shall be thrown into the lions' den. Now, O king, issue the decree and put it in writing so that it cannot be altered—in accordance with the laws of the Medes and Persians, which cannot be repealed." So King Darius put the decree in writing.
>
> Now when Daniel learned that the decree had been published, he went home to his upstairs room where the windows opened toward Jerusalem. Three times a day he got down on his knees

and prayed, giving thanks to his God, just as he had done before. Then these men went as a group and found Daniel praying and asking God for help (Daniel 6: 5–11).

Great people of God recognize their need for fellowship with the Heavenly Father and make it a priority.

The Purpose of a Daily Quiet Time

A daily quiet time with God should be your priority for four reasons.

TO GIVE DEVOTION TO GOD

Your daily time is not just a time to get from God, but also a time to give to God. God desires our devotion (see John 4:23). The Psalmist instructs: "Give unto the LORD the glory due unto his name; worship the LORD in the beauty of holiness" (Psalm 29:2, KJV). God is worthy and deserves our devotion. King Hezekiah was successful because everything he did was done in a spirit of complete devotion to God (see 2 Chronicles 31:21). We demonstrate our devotion and dedication to God by setting aside time each day to spend in His presence.

TO GET DIRECTION FROM GOD

In our times of prayer, Scripture reading, and meditation, God often will give us direction. "Show me the path where I should go, O Lord; point out the right road for me to walk. Lead me" (Psalm 25:4, *The Living Bible*). God cares about every detail of your life. As you look to God for direction, you can do two things:

1. **Consider your way.** As you pray, consider the decisions you have made and the decisions you face. According to the Book of Proverbs, this will result in God giving direction to your plans. "Ponder the path of thy feet, and let all thy ways be established" (Proverbs 4:26, KJV). "In all thy ways acknowledge him, and he shall direct thy paths" (Proverbs 3:6, KJV).

2. **Commit your day.** When you commit your schedule to the Lord, it helps you to be more flexible and not get bent out of shape when things don't go the way you think they should. Psalm 37:5 says, "Commit everything you do to the Lord. Trust him to help you do it and he will" (*The Living Bible*). As you pray, commit the plans of your day to God.

To Gain Delight in God

A scholarly Bible study is designed to study about Christ; a quiet time is designed to know Christ and spend time with Him. If you "delight thyself also in the LORD... he shall give thee the desires of thine heart" (Psalm 37:4, KJV). As we spend time in the presence of the Lord, we find peace, comfort, strength, and joy. It is difficult to establish any habit, but you will learn to love and look forward to your daily quiet time.

To Grow Daily Like God

God's purpose for our life is to make us like His Son—Christlikeness. As we spend time with the Father, He even promises to produce in us His character!

> For as you know him better, he will give you, through his great power, everything you need for living a truly good life: he even shares his own glory and his own goodness with us! And by that same mighty power he has given us all the other rich and wonderful blessings he promised; for instance, the promise to save us from the lust and rottenness all around us, and to give us his own character (2 Peter 1:3,4 *The Living Bible*).

As we grow in our knowledge of Him and relationship with Him, we begin to take on His nature. It will even become obvious to others around us. In Acts 4, Peter and John are brought before the Jewish leaders to answer for their faith. "When the Council saw the boldness of Peter and John,...they were amazed and realized what being with Jesus had done for them" (Acts 4:13, *The Living Bible*). When you spend daily time with Jesus, other people will notice the changes in your life.

The Practice of a Quiet Time

Many people who have been Christians for years have never been given practical instruction for having a quite time. They have heard Sunday school teachers teach and pastors preach that they need to have daily devotions. But no one has ever told them how to do it. We must teach people a simple procedure they can use in their daily time. The following principles will help you as you establish your habit.

SCHEDULE YOUR QUIET TIME AT THE SAME TIME EVERY DAY

The best time to have a quiet time is different for different individuals. For some it may be in the evening; for most it will be in the morning. In the morning you are more likely to be rested, your mind is less cluttered, and it is often the quietest time of the day. Many characters in the Bible rose early to meet with God. Abraham, Jacob, Moses, Hannah, Job, Hezekiah, David, Daniel, Ezekiel, and Jesus—all chose to begin the day with prayer. It is logical to begin the day with prayer. Beginning every day with prayer demonstrates that meeting with God is the first priority of your day. Whenever you choose to establish your time, give the best part of your day to God. Choose a time when you are alert, and schedule the same time each day. Be consistent.

Many teachers teach that you must spend 1 to 2 hours every day in devotions. The Bible is not specific about the length of a quiet time. Do you remember the first time you resolved to pray for a whole hour? If you are like most people, you prayed through your list in 5 minutes and then began to watch the clock, wondering how you could ever fill an hour. You may have left feeling guilty that you couldn't concentrate for the whole hour. Emphasize the quality of your time with God. There is no heavenly reward allocated for length of devotions. You can start with 15 minutes and allow your time to grow as you develop the habit. Resist the impulse to watch the clock and measure your prayer progress. Instead, enjoy the time you spend. As you continue the habit, you will find yourself spending more time each day.

HAVE YOUR QUIET TIME IN THE SAME PLACE EVERY DAY

Choose a special place where you pray each day. Jesus went to the Mount of Olives often for His prayer time (see Luke 22:39). It was a habit for Him. You need a place where you can be alone, without interruption. For some, their place may be in the backyard. For others, it may be a room at the church or even a closet in their home. Select a place that becomes your special place for fellowship with the Father.

GATHER THE RESOURCES YOU WILL NEED

What do you need for your quiet time? Following is a simple checklist:

- A Bible with comfortably readable print.
- A notebook to write down everything that you feel the Lord is speaking to you and to record your prayer list.
- A songbook or praise tape. Worship and singing is a wonderful way to spend time with God. Praise and worship music creates a wonderful atmosphere for devotions.

BEGIN WITH THE RIGHT ATTITUDES

Three attitudes will make your quiet time effective:

1. **Reverence.** You cannot rush into God's presence. Prepare your heart. Psalm 46:10 records God's instruction: "Be still, and know that I am God" (KJV).
2. **Expectancy.** Expect God to speak to you each day. The Psalmist prayed, "Open my eyes to see wonderful things in your Word" (Psalm 119:18, *The Living Bible*).
3. **Willingness to obey.** God will reveal things to you. You must be willing to obey His directions. Jesus said, "If any of you really determines to do God's will, then you will certainly know" (John 7:17, *The Living Bible*).

FOLLOW A SIMPLE PLAN

There is no formula that must be followed for your quiet time. However, you will find your time to be more effective if you develop a plan for your time. The following simple, 15-minute plan can serve as an example.

- Relax (1 minute). Be still and be quiet. Slow down. Prepare your heart. Prepare to wait on God. Get comfortable and forget the pressures of the day so that you can focus on God for the next 14 minutes.
- Read (4 minutes). Read systematically. Begin reading where you left off the day before. Read until you feel God is emphasizing something to you. Then stop and think about it. Do not worry about the number of chapters or verses you read each day. Instead, resolve to learn something each day. Reading with a set goal in mind often reduces your comprehension level.
- Reflect (4 minutes). Begin to meditate on the Scripture verses you have read. Meditation is the key to discovering how to apply Scripture to your life. Meditation is essentially thought digestion. You take a thought God gives you, put it in your mind, and think on it over and over again. Scriptural meditation is reading a passage in the Bible, then concentrating on it in different ways. Pick out one passage or verse you feel God is trying to teach you and do these five things:

  1. *Picture it.* Visualize the scene in your mind. Imagine yourself in the historical context. What would you have done in the situation? How would you have responded? What emotions would you have experienced if you had been there?
  2. *Pronounce it.* Say the verse aloud, each time emphasizing a different word (see Philippians 4:13). Each emphasis gives you a slightly different impression.
  3. *Paraphrase it.* Rewrite the verse in your own words.

4. *Personalize it.* Replace the pronouns or people in the verse with your own name.

5. *Pray it.* Turn the verse into a prayer and pray it back to God.[17]

- Record (2 minutes). Write a personal application statement that is practical, possible, and measurable. Ask yourself, what did this verse mean to the original hearers? What is the underlying, timeless principle? Where or how could I practice that principle? Record your thoughts, reflections, and responses in a journal. It will become a personal record of your spiritual journey.

- Request (4 minutes). Conclude your quiet time by talking to God about what He has shown you and making requests from your prayer list.

This plan is just one example of how you can structure your quiet time. If you intend to spend 30 minutes each day, adjust the times spent in each area accordingly.[18]

Common Difficulties in Having a Quiet Time

Most Christians are aware they should have a daily time of prayer and Bible study. Yet many of them struggle with developing the habit. What are some of the reasons people do not have a daily quiet time?

THE PROBLEM OF FOCUS

Many people have good intentions. They head to their special place to spend an hour with God. However, once they begin their prayer time, they begin to remember details and tasks that are ahead of them that day. Other people become too comfortable and fall asleep or daydream. If you struggle in this way, try walking when you pray. Write down the things about the day ahead to get them off your mind. Vary your praying—pray aloud for a while; sing a praise song. Change your prayer-time routine. Keep it fresh.

THE PROBLEM OF FATIGUE

The most difficult dilemma for many determined believers is in getting out of bed each morning. Remember when you made your resolutions for the New Year? Maybe you decided to exercise every day. But the first day was New Year's Day. Who exercises on a holiday? The second day was your first day back to work and the kids' first day back to school. You could not imagine exercising on that day. Before you knew it, the middle of spring had arrived and you still were not exercising! Developing the discipline of a daily quiet time is no different. Determine to get up and have your quiet time regardless of how fatigued you may be. Go to bed an hour earlier; quit watching late-night television—do whatever it takes to keep your appointment with God.

THE PROBLEM OF FEARING FAILURE

Some people are afraid to start a quiet time because they have tried many times and failed. Don't give up! Paul encouraged the church in the Book of Galatians: "We will reap a harvest of blessing if we don't get discouraged and give up" (Galatians 6:9, *The Living Bible*). Some counselors teach that it takes as many as 16 weeks to completely ingrain a behavior. Resolve to develop your habit over the course of time.

THE PROBLEM OF FRUITLESSNESS

Sometimes it may feel like you are just not getting anything out of your quiet time. Your prayers are not being answered. You don't feel the presence of God as strong as before. Job surely felt like his prayers were not being heard. He had lost his children, his possessions, his health, and his friends. His words were those of a man who had given up:

The arrows of the Almighty are in me, my spirit drinks in their poison; God's terrors are marshaled against me.... Oh, that I might have my request, that God... loose his hand and cut me off!... What strength do I have, that I should still hope? What prospects, that I should be patient?... Do I have any power to help myself, now that success has been driven from me? (Job 6:4,8,9,11,13).

Job displayed faith despite fruitless seeming prayers, saying, "Though he slay me, yet will I hope in him" (Job 13:15).

Do not trust your feelings! You may be tired, in a hurry, or in a time of testing. But God will reward you for your faithfulness. After Job had prayed for his friends, the Lord made him prosperous again and gave him twice as much as he had before. "The LORD blessed the latter part of Job's life more than the first.... After this, Job lived a hundred and forty years; he saw his children and their children to the fourth generation. And so he died, old and full of years" (Job 42:12–17).

THE PROBLEM OF FAULTY COMPARISONS

One of the biggest hurdles to maintaining a daily quiet time is faulty comparisons. Who among us is not inspired by the stories of Praying Hyde and Smith Wigglesworth? These men prayed for hours every day and fasted and prayed for weeks on end. We are inspired by the stories of these great men, but intimidated at the idea of duplicating their efforts. Many people never begin a quiet time because they think God expects marathon prayer sessions. Thank God for great men and women who have dedicated their lives to prayer! But God has also called some to evangelism, teaching, preaching, serving, etc. Prayer must be a part of each of our lives, but not all of us will be called to periods of lengthy prayer.

When you compare yourself to someone better than you, guilt can set in. When you compare yourself to someone worse than you, pride has an opening. Instead of comparing yourself to others, do your very best to honor God in your prayer life.

THE PROBLEM OF FICTION

Satan continually attempts to deceive the believer. People struggle with maintaining their quiet time when they begin to believe the devil's fiction. He wants you to believe that God does not love you. Satan tries to convince you that it is all a waste of time, that your prayers will never be answered. He tries to make us believe that God can't hear and respond to all of our prayers at the same time.

Recognize such fiction is a tool of the enemy. If he can convince you to become lackadaisical in your devotional life, he has greatly hindered your effectiveness as a Christian. Instead of believing Satan's lies, turn to God's Word for His timeless truths. When Satan says, "God doesn't love you," quote John 3:16. When Satan tries to convince you that God doesn't hear your prayers, turn to God's Word for the truth:

> Since we have a great high priest who has gone through the heavens, Jesus the Son of God, let us hold firmly to the faith we profess. For we do not have a high priest who is unable to sympathize with our weaknesses, but we have one who has been tempted in every way, just as we are—yet was without sin. Let us then approach the throne of grace with confidence, so that we may receive mercy and find grace to help us in our time of need (Hebrews 4:14–16).

Refuse to believe the lies of the devil!

The Problem of Folly

We are surrounded by the folly of the world. Multitudes of things vie for our attention. It is difficult to set aside time for daily devotions when the world is offering so many alternatives. We are bombarded every day by television, radio, the Internet, countless entertainment events and opportunities. The glitz and glamour of the entertainment industry can make prayer and fasting appear mundane. Americans are addicted to amusement. The root word of amusement is *muse*, which means "thinking." *A-muse* means "not thinking." We have become accustomed to activities that require little or no input from us. To make a daily quiet time a habit, we must beware of the nonthinking mode of amusement.

Personal Devotion and Teaching

Pam agreed to begin teaching the sixth-grade girls Sunday school class. She was handed a quarterly, a teacher's guide, and a sample lesson plan and told to be ready the next Sunday. She was excited! She was determined to be an excellent teacher. Her lesson preparation took 5 hours each week. Balancing the preparation time with the needs of her family and job became difficult. She tried studying late at night but woke up tired each morning. She even tried using her lunch hour at work but was constantly distracted and interrupted. Finally, she began using her personal devotion time each morning to work on the next week's lesson. It couldn't hurt. After all, she was teaching the class for God. Although she was not using her quiet-time plan, she was *still* spending time in the Word of God. In neglecting her personal spiritual development, Pam made a mistake that many others have made.

A common error of teachers and leaders is the thought that lesson or sermon preparation takes the place of personal devotions. There is a difference. Every teacher, preacher, and leader must develop and maintain a quiet time to ensure their relationship with God is fresh, current, and powerful. Preparation time can never take the place of personal time. In lesson preparation, you seek to ensure the lesson is understandable and applicable to the students. The focus of the preparation is the needs, maturity level, and development of the class. In a quiet time, you seek to apply the Scriptures personally and to hear God for your own life. The focus is on your needs, maturity level, and development. We must always be growing at the same rate as our students. It is a fallacy to believe we can continue to lead others to maturity even as we neglect our own.

Your personality, charisma, wit, or charm is not what qualifies you to lead others. You are effective in teaching others what you have learned and experienced for yourself. To lead others into a mature, committed, personal relationship with Jesus Christ, your relationship must also be mature, committed, and personal. For the mature believer, there is no greater joy than the daily time in fellowship with Christ. In His presence, there is renewal, refreshing, and a continual refilling.

Use the following questions to evaluate your personal devotional life:

- Do I spend time in prayer, Bible reading, and meditation a minimum of 5 days each week?
- Do I have a plan or procedure that directs my devotional time?
- Am I able to eliminate distractions and focus on God in my quiet time?
- Is it obvious to others that I spend time with Jesus?
- Do I look forward to my quiet time, or do I consider it an obligation?

4
A Climate
for Maturity

To lead people into a mature relationship with Jesus Christ, you must understand several areas. First, it is important to know the characteristics of a mature believer and an immature believer. You cannot lead someone into maturity unless you understand the definition of maturity. Second, you must understand how to lead. Many people are armed with volumes of useful information and possess all the knowledge necessary to disciple others. However, some of these same individuals do not possess the necessary leadership skills to accomplish the process. Every teacher should become more than a teacher. Every teacher should also be a leader. Paul, in his letter to the Corinthians, summed up the role of leadership in maturity, saying, "Follow my example, as I follow the example of Christ" (1 Corinthians 11:1). It is our task to lead others as Christ leads us. A basic understanding of leadership principles will greatly enhance your teaching and discipling.

If you are frustrated in your efforts to disciple others, if you feel like your followers are not following, become a leader. The proverb sums it up well: If you are leading but no one is following, all you are doing is taking a walk. There are many different definitions of leadership.

- Leadership is taking people from where they are to where they need to be, and when they arrive, they believe it was their idea.
- Leadership is a dynamic process in which a man or woman with God-given capacity influences a specific group of God's people toward His purposes for the group.[19]
- Leadership is getting people to work for you because they want to.
- Leadership is leading people.

Whatever definition you choose, all agree with John Maxwell when he says leadership is influence.

Leadership Maxim #1: Effective Leaders Must Be Empowered by the Holy Spirit

Many practical leadership principles can be learned. You can attend seminars, purchase books and tapes, and hone your leadership abilities. Learn everything you can. However, people will never reach spiritual maturity and your leadership will never reach its full potential without the divine empowerment of the Holy Spirit. Jesus himself emphasized the role of the Holy Spirit in leadership:

> When he, the Spirit of truth, comes, he will guide you into all truth. He will not speak on his own; he will speak only what he hears, and he will tell you what is yet to come. He will bring glory to me by taking from what is mine and making it known to you. All that belongs to the Father is mine. That is why I said the Spirit will take from what is mine and make it known to you (John 16:13–15).

The Holy Spirit reveals truth. As a teacher you must depend on the Holy Spirit. Nobody else has the total knowledge of all your gifts and abilities. The disciples, in Acts 2, already possessed the gift of evangelism. However, that gift was not fully revealed in their ministry until after their Holy Spirit baptism. Your leadership potential will blossom when you realize the foundation of all leadership skills is the anointing of the Holy Spirit.

In addition, your students will never reach full maturity in Christ without the baptism in the Holy Spirit. It is fundamental to development. The Great Commission is not the first command that Jesus gave the church. First He told His disciples to go to Jerusalem and wait until they received power from on high (see Luke 24:49). He had no desire to launch them into ministry until they had experienced a powerful encounter with the Holy Spirit.

Leadership Maxim #2: Leadership Is a Role, Not a Title

When you became a teacher, you were handed a quarterly, a class list, and a Sunday school policy and assigned a room. The moment you were announced to your class, you became the teacher. However, although you became the teacher, you may not have become the leader. Leadership is not a title. Leadership is a role.

The one who has the most followers is the leader. Consider the example of a junior high boys Sunday school class. Jim was appointed the new teacher. He walked in the first morning to the sight of 14 seventh and eighth graders engaged in a massive spitball war. Paper was flying, chairs were overturned; the room was a disaster! The noise level approached that of a jet airplane during takeoff. Jim laid aside his carefully prepared lesson and screamed at the top of his lungs. The boys turned in shock. Who was this man telling them he was going to get the pastor? The boys stopped for a moment, and then one redheaded little boy shouted: "Get him!" The boys turned their fire to Jim, their new teacher. Jim ran from the room, chased by a barrage of spitballs. Jim was the teacher, but the redheaded runt was the leader.

You are not a leader because of a position or title. You are a leader when your influence has reached the point where your students willingly follow your direction. Too many teachers fail to recognize the importance of building influence in their class. Authority without influence is like trying to push a rope.

Leadership Maxim #3: Leaders Do "the Right Thing"

Leaders do "the right thing" regardless of personal convenience or comfort. In the Book of 2 Samuel, Uzzah did what seemed a good thing, but it was not the right thing.

> He and all his men set out from Baalah of Judah to bring up from there the ark of God.... They set the ark of God on a new cart and brought it from the house of Abinadab, which was on the hill. Uzzah and Ahio, sons of Abinadab, were guiding the new cart with the ark of God on it, and Ahio was walking in front of it. David and the whole house of Israel were celebrating with all their might before the Lord, with songs and with harps, lyres, tambourines, sistrums and cymbals. When they came to the threshing floor of Nacon, Uzzah reached out and took hold of the ark of God, because the oxen stumbled. The Lord's anger burned against Uzzah because of his irreverent act; therefore God struck him down and he died there beside the ark of God (2 Samuel 6:2–7).

God's instruction was that no one should touch the ark. Uzzah was afraid the ark would fall and perhaps be damaged. He reached out to steady the ark, and God got angry. Uzzah was killed because he did not do the right thing.

Thank God that we do not live in Old Testament times! How many of us would be struck down for neglecting the right thing? As a teacher you may teach your class the value of self-help techniques. It is a good thing for your students to discover the abilities that enable them to recover from difficulties. However, if the emphasis on self-help is greater than the emphasis on God's delivering power, it becomes damaging to the spiritual development of the student.

Leaders do the right thing. Many difficulties are easily

resolved when personal convenience, preference, desires, schedules, and agendas are sacrificed in order to do right.

Leadership Maxim #4: Leadership Is Character Driven

Tyler, a four-year-old boy, intently listened to a portion of the Sunday message on obeying the law. That afternoon he got in the car with his father, the minister. As they were driving down the road, the radar detector began to beep. Tyler asked, "Dad, what is that noise?" His father replied, "It's my radar detector." Tyler pressed the issue. His next question was, "Dad, what does it do?" His father explained that a radar detector helps us know when police cars are nearby. Tyler's next question was, "Why do we want to know?" At that point Tyler's father realized he did not want to answer the question. Telling the truth to his son would be admitting he was intentionally breaking the law. He reached down, unplugged his radar detector, and threw it in the back seat. He looked at his son and said, "We don't need to know, son. I'm putting it away." He never used his radar detector again. What happened between Tyler and his dad? Tyler wanted to know if his dad's conduct was in agreement with his stated beliefs.

Leadership is character driven. Your actions must agree with your instructions. If you teach on tithing, you should be a tither. If you teach on integrity, you must always tell the truth. If you teach on purity, you must abstain from every appearance of evil. If you teach on anger, you must live a self-controlled life. If you teach on gossip, your conversations should be uplifting. Your life and your lips must agree.

Many teachers disqualify themselves and their leadership by failing to live a life of character. James tells us that leaders are subject to a higher standard: "Not many of you should presume to be teachers, my brothers, because you know that we who teach will be judged more strictly" (James 3:1). To lead effectively out of love, you must be willing to limit your options. For example, many teachers choose not to attend movies. Although they may not have a personal conviction regarding movies, they know that many movies contain objectionable material. Not wanting students to wonder which movie their teacher may have watched, the teacher chooses to avoid theaters.

What you do is often more important than what you say. Many times principles are more easily caught than taught. It is our role as leaders to model the character of Christ.

Leadership Maxim #5: Leaders Understand the Importance of Teamwork

Effective leaders understand that although they may be the most important person on a team, they are not important without the team. There are several important components of a team.

A Team Shares a Common Goal

Don Shula and Ken Blanchard in their book *Everyone's a Coach* stress the importance of goals. "Goal setting is important. All good performance starts with clear goals. Goals point people in the right direction. Goals begin the accomplishment process."[20]

Setting goals helps keep the focus of your class on the big picture. The goal of maturity will involve instruction in many areas, some exciting and some mundane. Your class will tolerate and even appreciate subjects that are mundane when they know the result will be maturity.

A Team Practices Open Communication

A team can become disjointed and confused if communication is lacking. An effective team leader continually informs the team of the task and objectives before them. Not only does the leader communicate with the team, but the team must also have the freedom to communicate with the leader. Corporations have gone bankrupt because the CEO was unaware of the difficulties on the factory floor. On an effective team, each member is able to give input and provide feedback.

A TEAM IS BUILT ON TRUST

Trust is the glue that keeps a team intact. A team without trust quickly disintegrates. A leader can never demand trust but, instead, earns the right to be trusted by consistency and loyalty. Each team member earns the trust of the team in the same manner.

TEAM MEMBERS PRACTICE ENCOURAGEMENT

Everyone enjoys being congratulated on a job well done. Team members seek to support others in their weaknesses so the whole team can be strengthened.

TEAMS MANAGE FAILURE WITH COMPASSION

Proverbs 24:16 states, "Though a righteous man falls seven times, he rises again." Even righteous people make mistakes. Team members recognize that failure is not a person, but an event. When one member fails, the other team members respond with compassion and forgiveness. They look at failure as a learning experience they can all benefit from.

TEAM MEMBERS FUNCTION IN DIFFERENT GIFTS

The Dallas Cowboys are a great football team. However, they would quickly become ineffective if Emmit Smith decided he wanted to be quarterback, and Troy Aikman decided to play defensive tackle. Both men are tremendously skilled football players. But they understand they have a specific role to play for the Dallas Cowboys. Their talent, abilities, experience, and personality determine their role. In a class there is only one teacher. But each student has a role to play and a contribution to make to the team. Understanding that role promotes peace, harmony, and effectiveness.

TEAMS EVALUATE PERFORMANCE

Four kinds of consequences can follow a person's performance:

1. **A positive consequence.** Something good occurs (from the person's perspective)—praise, recognition, a raise, or a bigger opportunity to perform. If a reward is given, the person is apt to repeat the action. People tend to move toward pleasure. Positive consequences motivate future behavior.

2. **Redirection.** Performance is stopped and the person's efforts are rechanneled to correct what was being done incorrectly. If a person is redirected to do something correctly, he or she is apt to continue doing it correctly. Redirection can be a powerful way to get people to change their behavior.

3. **A negative consequence.** Something bad occurs (from the person's perspective) for example, a reprimand, a punishment, a demotion, or a removal from an activity. People tend to move away from pain. If an action produces undesirable consequences, the person is apt to avoid it.

4. **No response.** Nothing is said or done following the action. Good actions that receive no recognition at all are apt to be discarded eventually; bad actions will continue unchanged. The only exception is when someone is self-actualizing—that is, they love what they're doing and will continue to do it well regardless of whether they receive any recognition. Performance is most influenced by consequences—that is, the response from a coach who is on the scene.[21]

Many teachers and leaders neglect the process of evaluation because they fear offending others. Evaluation is essential to improving performance. A definition of insanity is "to keep doing what you've always done and expect different results." You must evaluate, retool, try again, and then reevaluate to ensure continual growth.

Leadership Maxim #6: Leadership Is Not Necessarily Ministry

Ministry is serving God by helping others through the work of your own hands. Performing the task yourself brings fulfillment. Leadership is serving God by equipping others to use their hands to help people. The leader finds fulfillment in enabling others to minister effectively. A leader not only understands, but implements the process of equipping as explained in Ephesians 4:11,12.

Leadership Maxim #7: Leadership Is Not Management

There is a difference between leadership and management. Stephen Covey in his book *Principle-Centered Leadership* describes the contrast.

> Leadership deals with direction—with making sure that the ladder is leaning against the right wall. Management deals with speed. Leadership deals with vision—with keeping the mission in sight—and with effectiveness and results. Management deals with establishing structure and systems to get those results. Leadership focuses on the top line. Management focuses on the bottom line.[22]

Leading a class is more than maintaining a class list, calling absentees, and preparing the room. Those tasks are part of managing a class. Leading a class involves taking your students on the spiritual journey toward maturity.

Leadership Maxim #8: Leaders Rise to the Occasion

Much has been said, written, and studied concerning gifts and aptitudes. Leaders understand that when a crisis arises or a decision is required, they must act, regardless of their personal limitations. A leader has a "whatever it takes" attitude.

What basketball fan will forget Magic Johnson in the final game of the 1980 NBA finals? Magic was a point guard; his job was to handle the ball and run the offense. The Lakers' Hall of Fame center, Kareem Abdul-Jabbar, was injured. The Lakers had no reliable backup center. The sportswriters, commentators, and analysts all predicted the team's defeat. What they hadn't taken into account was a leader with a "whatever it takes" attitude. Magic, beginning his legendary point-guard career, volunteered to play center. Fans were amazed. The television commentators were astounded that a point guard knew how to shoot a skyhook, the shot Kareem had made famous. That night, Magic Johnson scored 42 points and the Lakers won the championship. Magic was selected Most Valuable Player of the championship series, and his place as leader of the Lakers was secured.

Who will be the Most Valuable Player in your church? Will it be you? The Most Valuable Player will be the one who is willing to step in and lead when the situation requires a leader. You may not feel you have the right gifts or talents, but when you step outside your comfort zone, God honors your faith. In the New Testament, Paul had a "whatever it takes" attitude. He recognized that his weaknesses when packaged with God's strength became assets. He wrote: "But he [God] said to me, 'My grace is sufficient for you, for my power is made perfect in weakness.' Therefore I will boast all the more gladly about my weaknesses, so that Christ's power may rest on me" (2 Corinthians 12:9).

> Paul was so confident in God's faithfulness and love, in His promises, and in what Christ had accomplished for him at the cross, that he was willing to risk failure. His confidence in Christ freed him to glory in his humanity that was being conformed to Christ. Paul had no fear of failure because he had no fear of his potential to fail. He could accept his inevitable weaknesses because he understood that God's grace had already covered them all. In fact, Paul's weaknesses were the very channels through which the power of Christ could be manifested in his life. And our weaknesses are the very channels through which the power of the risen Christ can be manifested through our lives![23]

Do not be afraid to venture into the unknown. James Bryant Conant said, "Behold the turtle: He only makes progress when he sticks his neck out." The path to spiritual success is often paved with uncertain steps. Those steps often involve risk. Remember, you can "do all things through Christ who strengthens you" (see Philippians 4:13).

Leadership Maxim #9: Leaders Are Visionary

A clear vision and a set of operating values is really just a picture of what things would look like if everything was running as planned and the vision was being fulfilled. World-class athletes often visualize themselves breaking a world record, pitching a perfect game, or making a 99-yard punt return. They know that power comes from having a clear mental picture of their best performance potential.[24]

Vision is the method God uses to motivate people to grow closer to Him. You will never accomplish great things for God if you are satisfied with the status quo. Vision directs our footsteps toward growth.

Effective teachers have God's vision for their classes. "Ultimately God's set of goals must be sought, not the desires of your heart or the fruits of your natural abilities, even if the intent is to please Him."[25]

How do you get God's vision for your ministry?

- Understand your purpose.
- Evaluate the need.
- Listen to the Holy Spirit.
- Seek the advice of spiritual authority.
- Listen to the people who have your best interest at heart.

Leadership Maxim #10: Leaders Are Listeners

"Dr. S. S. Hayakawa says, 'We can, if we are able to listen as well as to speak, become better informed and wiser as we grow older, instead of being stuck like some people with the same little bundle of prejudices at 65 that we had at 25.'"[26]

A good listener encourages others to communicate their feelings. It is difficult for students to communicate what they are really thinking and feeling. They do not want to be rejected, hurt, contradicted, or embarrassed. In today's society many young people have a fatalistic view, believing "no one really cares what I think anyway—it's not going to change the future." An effective leader is able to encourage students to reveal their true hurts, feelings, and needs.

How effective would your teaching be if you knew exactly what your students were feeling? Consider how your lessons would change if you understood the fears of your students. You may have never been a latchkey child. Your parents may not have gone through an ugly divorce. You may have never had a close friend overdose on drugs or commit suicide. How can you empathize with situations you have never encountered? You develop empathy by listening to the hurts, needs, hopes, fears, and dreams of others. Listen with a perceptive heart. Ask God to enlarge your understanding. Tuned-in teachers should be able to identify the greatest needs of their classes.

Qualities of a Leader

What are some qualities of a leader? What characteristics, attitudes, and behaviors should a leader have?

1. **A leader values corporate good over personal preference.** A leader supports all programs and ministries of the church, regardless of personal preference. Every other member of the ministry team sees the leader as an ally.

2. **A leader is never satisfied with his or her spiritual condition, but is always seeking to grow**. All leaders are learners. When leaders quit learning, they quit leading. A leader is genuinely committed to personal spiritual development.

3. **A leader has a genuine passion for the lost.** A leader's passion for the lost is evidenced in giving, sharing, and praying. A lack of concern for the sinner disqualifies a leader. God's actions at Calvary exemplify His concern for the lost.

4. **A leader serves willingly, and complains rarely.** Whiners make poor leaders! A leader attends to the task at hand, without complaining.

5. **A leader accepts everyone, and shuns no one.** Those who rule by exclusion make poor leaders. They polarize the group, destroy harmony, and create ill will. A leader seeks to include all. Everyone may not have a buddy in the leader, but they do have a leader.

6. **A leader is sensitive to others.** Leaders place a high priority on the feelings of others. They genuinely care about their classes.

7. **A leader avoids the appearance of evil.** You cannot mold others without modeling. Those you are leading scrutinize your every action.

8. **A leader worships enthusiastically.** God loves to be praised! A leader worships in "spirit and in truth."

9. **A leader participates in everything, even when it's not a personal preference.** The spirit of cooperation is vital to a team. A leader will support personalities and activities whether or not they are particularly enjoyable.

10. **A leader is proactive, not reactive.** When your first action is a reaction, it is usually wrong. Leaders seek to make change, not react to change.

11. **A leader readily apologizes when wrong.** There is power in the apology! A sincere, honest apology ends conflict.

12. **A leader is faithful in all aspects of church life.** A leader attends Sunday morning, Sunday night, and midweek services.

13. **A leader is punctual.** You cannot expect from your students what you are not willing to do yourself. If you are habitually late to church, do not complain when your students are late to class!

14. **A leader is accountable.** A leader welcomes a climate of accountability and seeks to establish relationships with those in authority.

15. **A leader has a tender heart.** A leader is open and sensitive to the working of the Holy Spirit, fearing hardness of heart almost as much as sin.

16. **A leader strives for excellence.** A leader refuses to settle for the ordinary but looks to create excellence in every area. Your effort may not produce the best, but it should be your best!

17. **A leader resolves conflict.** A leader is a peacemaker. Slow to blame others and quick to take responsibility, such a leader looks to heal relationships.

18. **A leader chooses friends wisely.** Birds of a feather flock together—your mother may have said it, but it is still true. Paul says, "Bad company corrupts good character" (1 Corinthians 15:33).

19. **A leader's word is good.** "Lies will get any man into trouble, but honesty is its own defense" (Proverbs 12:13, *The Living Bible*).

20. **A leader is loving.** Jesus said our love is the test of our discipleship: "By this all men will know that you are my disciples, if you love one another" (John 13:35).

21. **A leader effects change.** A leader is continually seeking to improve programs and performance, being unsatisfied with the status quo.

22. **A leader is a servant.** The most effective leadership is servant leadership.

23. **A leader loves family**. Leaders understand the importance of their own family and home, seeking to balance ministry responsibilities and family responsibilities.

24. **A leader shares the faith.** We are all called to be a witness. You do not have to have the gift of evangelism to be a soul winner.

25. **A leader has leaders and respects them.** If you do not respect your leaders, your followers will not respect you.

5
Communicating
for Maturity

The Process of Teaching for Maturity

The Christian life is more than belief, it is also behavior. It is more than a creed, it is also character. James 1:22 says, "Do not merely listen to the word,... Do what it says." D. L. Moody once said: "The Bible was not given to increase our knowledge, it was given to change our lives." When preparing to teach, you must prepare with the goal of maturity in mind. Students should leave class transformed as well as informed!

In many instances, a teacher is given a quarterly and completely relies on its instructions. However, to lead your students toward maturity, you must tailor each lesson to your individual students. The wise teacher uses the curriculum as a guide, adapting each week's lesson to the needs of the students. Each week, as you prepare your lesson, consider the following questions. They will help ensure that your teaching is practical, life applicational, and leading to growth in others.

QUESTION #1: WHO IS MY AUDIENCE?

Whether you are a pastor, Sunday school teacher, or any other kind of public speaker, your first question must be, Who is my audience? First Corinthians 9:22,23 gives us this first step:

> When I am with those whose consciences bother them easily, I don't act as though I know it all and don't say they are foolish; the result is that they are willing to let me help them. Yes, whatever a person is like, I try to find common ground with him so that he will let me tell him about Christ and let Christ save him. I do this to get the Gospel to them and also for the blessing I myself receive when I see them come to Christ (*The Living Bible*).

Your first step is to understand how your audience thinks. Jesus was very effective with people because He understood them. On occasion the Gospels say, "Jesus knew their thoughts." Jesus was always aware of the individuals who were before Him.

When you are considering your audience, think about these four important questions:

- What makes them laugh?
- What makes them cry?
- What occupies their time?
- What do they lack?

If you can determine what makes someone laugh, you know his or her level of happiness. If you can determine what makes someone cry, you know his or her level of pain. If you can determine what occupies their time, you know their interests. If you can determine what they lack, you know their needs. If you neglect your students' challenges, problems, and stresses, if you miss their pain, if you miss what interests them, you lose the ability to reach them at the point of their need. They may want to know how God will make a difference in their businesses or in their homes, in their classes or in their jobs. If that is their interest, they will not enjoy a dissertation on the Dead Sea Scrolls. Paul gives us some helpful instructions regarding teaching to the needs of our students: "When you talk, do not say harmful things. But say what people need—words that will help others become stronger. Then what you say will help those who listen to you" (Ephesians 4:29, NCV).

In communication the hearer is constantly asking, What does this mean to me? You are probably asking the same question as you read this chapter: How will this information help me? The purpose of teaching is to move people from where they are to where Christ wants them to be. Effective teaching often starts with a need, addressing an area of concern in the student's life.

Lesson preparation is a weekly struggle for many people because they are asking themselves the wrong question. The wrong question is—What should I teach about this week? The right question is—Who will I be teaching this week? If you can figure out your audience and their needs, you will get a good idea about what God has for you to say. When a parent walks into your class and says, "My daughter is on drugs; my son has turned his back on God" and you are in the midst of an 8-week lecture on archaeology and the Bible, she may not return. The Dead Sea Scrolls are important, but you can begin by relating to the needs, the pain, of your students.

QUESTION #2: WHAT DOES THE BIBLE SAY ABOUT YOUR STUDENTS' PROBLEMS?

Now that you have identified the problems of your students, the second question to ask yourself is, What does the Bible say about their problems? Is there an answer to their problems in the Bible? For every problem, there is a corresponding promise. Find all the verses on the problem you have selected. Use your concordance and every translation. Find out how the Word of God addresses the problem. Remember, we are trying to address the problems of the audience before us, just like Jesus did! Jesus started where the people were; He did not start with His own agenda.

What is the purpose of the Bible? All Scripture is inspired by God and useful for teaching the faith, correcting error, resetting the direction of life, training in good living. The ultimate purpose of the Bible is not to teach biblical archaeology or just doctrinal facts. The ultimate purpose of the Bible is to transform character, to produce Christlikeness in a person. Therefore, teaching must always be related to life, even when you are teaching doctrine. It is important to teach on the Holy Spirit. But you must relate that teaching to life. He is not an obscure spirit, like Dickens' Ghost of Christmas Yet to Come. He is not some cloud with an eye. The Holy Spirit is a person, who desires intimacy and wants to communicate with you.

It is not our task to make the Bible relevant, it is relevant! It is our task to show its relevance. How do we show its relevance? We illustrate the relevance of God's Word by applying it to today's problems.

QUESTION #3: HOW WILL I SAY IT SO IT MAKES SENSE?

There are thousands of baseball pitchers in America. They all stand the same distance from home plate: 60 feet and 6 inches. They all throw the same size ball. But the difference between a major leaguer and an amateur is delivery. Delivery is an important part of the process of teaching. After determining what the Bible says about your student's needs, ask yourself, How can I say it so my students can understand it? How will I say it so it makes sense? How can I make it practical to them? Regardless of the age you are teaching, it is your responsibility to communicate the truths of God's Word on a level they can understand.

Christianity is a lifestyle. Teaching is focused on teaching people how to live. The result of sound teaching is character, a difference in the lifestyle of the learner. It is not enough to simply interpret the text. It must be applied in a practical way. Interpretation without application is useless.

As you study the New Testament, you realize that it is almost entirely application. Consider the Sermon on the Mount.

How much of it is practical? Every verse is life applicational; 100 percent is practical. The Book of James is application, a guide to living the Christian life. Even the Book of Romans, perhaps the most doctrinal book in the Bible, is half application. Eight chapters focus on doctrine, the other eight focus on application. Ephesians is half application and half doctrine. Colossians is half doctrine and half application. Galatians is almost all application. Paul continually balanced his teaching between doctrine and duty, between belief and behavior. Why is the Word of God still relevant after hundreds of years? It deals with life.

Jesus did not say, "I have come that you might have information." He said, "I have come that you might have life" (see John 10:10). Without application, your lessons become merely a harmless discussion. Life application should be our goal every week. If you cannot find the life application in the scheduled lesson, find a new lesson.

If you want your teaching to make sense, here are some helpful guidelines:

1. Determine what you want your students to do. What specifically should be their response? The Great Commission says, "Teach them to *do* everything I commanded you" (see Matthew 28:20), not "teach them to remember." At times, suggest a practical assignment.
2. Discuss the reason they should do it. Why should I make this change in my life? What will it do for me? Explain the benefits of the change and the drawbacks of refusing to change.
3. Demonstrate how to do it. Peter's sermon at Pentecost is a perfect example. It begins with his audience's questions and ends with an application. The question that started the sermon was, "What does this mean?" (Acts 2:12). At the end of Peter's answer, the people asked, "What shall we do?" And Peter replied, "Repent and be baptized" (Acts 2:37,38).

Teachers must show their students how to apply the message. Provide your class with a step-by-step procedure. Nothing becomes dynamic until you become specific. People are looking for practical answers.

At the end of every message, every class session, your students should not have to ask this question: "Yes, but how?" We teach, "You need to be a good father." Yes, but how? "You need to be godly." Yes, but how? "You need to have a devotional life." Yes, but how? We must always answer the "how" question. Exhortation without explanation leads to frustration. We should balance our "ought to" teaching with "how to" teaching.

QUESTION #4: WHAT IS THE MOST POSITIVE WAY TO SAY IT?

After determining the problems of your class members, what God's Word says about it, and how you can communicate it in a way they can understand, determine the most positive way to say it. The Bible tells us that speaking in a positive way increases our persuasiveness. "The wise of heart is called perceptive, and pleasant speech increases persuasiveness" (Proverbs 16:21, NRSV).

Too many preachers and teachers say things in a negative manner. You don't lift people up by putting them down. Does nagging work on you? No, criticism only makes people defensive. Jesus said, "I did not come to condemn the world, but to save it" (see John 3:17) The Holy Spirit is the agent of conviction, not the teacher. When you are abrasive, you are never persuasive. Colossians 4:5,6 gives good instruction: "Make the most of your chances to tell others the Good News. Be wise in all your contacts with them. Let your conversation be gracious as well as sensible, for then you will have the right answer for everyone" (*The Living Bible*).

Jesus came to preach good news. When you are preparing a lesson, ask yourself: Is this lesson good news? Do you still teach against sin? Of course. The problem is, we have sinned; the promise is, we can be forgiven. "For the wages of sin is death; but the gift of God is eternal life through Jesus Christ our Lord" (Romans 6:23, KJV). You can teach against adultery or you can teach on how to affair-proof your marriage. Promote the positive alternative! Show people how to change!

How then do you teach on a negative passage? Teach on a negative passage with a humble, loving attitude. Don't teach on hell like you are glad people are going there. When you teach on a negative subject, put yourself in the same boat as your students. Be transparent, open and honest. Confess where you have fallen short. Instead of saying "You need to..." say "We need to...".

QUESTION #5: WHAT IS THE MOST ENCOURAGING WAY TO SAY IT?

After determining the most positive way to share your message, determine the most encouraging manner you can say it in. Consider what the Bible says about encouragement: "Anxious hearts are very heavy but a word of encouragement does wonders!" (Proverbs 12:25, *The Living Bible*).

Every week you can count on people in your class having three fundamental needs:

1. They need to have their faith reinforced.
2. They need to have their hope renewed.
3. They need to have their love restored.

When you teach to broken hearts, you are always relevant. Your job is to infuse your students with new hope and remind them that with Christ no situation is hopeless. Encourage them. Relieve their pain; give them affirmation.

Jesus comforted the afflicted and afflicted the comfortable. Jesus said negative things to the sanctimonious Pharisees, not to the unchurched. Why did He put down the Pharisees? He did it because they were always saying negative things to everyone else. Don't be negative! Don't just tell it like it is. Everyone knows how it is. Tell it like it can be. Encouraging words create excitement in the mind of the listener.

QUESTION #6: WHAT IS THE MOST SIMPLE WAY TO SAY IT?

After determining the most positive and encouraging way to relate the Bible's answer to the needs of your class, determine the simplest way to say it. Paul spoke simply to his followers. He said, "When I came to you, brothers, I did not come with eloquence or superior wisdom as I proclaimed to you the testimony about God" (1 Corinthians 2:1).

Notice that Paul contrasts oratory with speaking simply. Later in the same chapter he says, "My preaching was very plain, not with a lot of oratory" (see verse 4). What is oratory? Oratory is simply dramatically stating what people already agree with. It is used to reinforce values that are already held, to restate beliefs that people already agree with. It is the old-fashioned way to communicate.

Jesus taught profound truths in simple ways. He would say, "Consider the lilies of the fields" (see Matthew 6:28) when teaching about worry. Many of us do the exact reverse. We teach simple truths in profound ways. Many times when we think we are being deep, we are just being muddy and confusing. Mark 12:37 says that "the common people heard him gladly" (author's paraphrase). If that is the way Jesus taught, that's the way we should teach. Charles Spurgeon said a sermon is like a well. "If there is anything in it, it appears bright and reflective." But he said, "If there is nothing in it, it appears dark, and deep, and mysterious."

It is easy to communicate the gospel. It is much more difficult to communicate it in a simple, easy-to-understand manner. Remember, the simplest things are often the strongest things! Albert Einstein once said, "You do not really understand something unless you can explain it to your grandmother." Do not be afraid of being called a simple teacher. There is a difference between being simple and being simplistic. Simple is saying, "This is the day the Lord has made, let us rejoice and be glad." Simplistic is saying, "Have a nice day." There is a big difference between the two. You can be brilliant, but if you cannot communicate it in a simple way, your wisdom is not worth much. The simple things communicate effectively. You can remember several things in keeping your message simple:

1. Condense the message into a single sentence. If you cannot say it in a sentence, your purpose probably is not very clear. Unless you know exactly where you are headed, the people are not going to be able to follow.

2. Keep your outline simple. A recent study revealed that the uninterested person can remember only two bits of information. An interested person can remember seven bits. Too much of anything loses its value. Keep your outline simple and restate the outline points many times.

3. Make your applications the points of your outline. Make your outline points action statements. If the only thing people may remember is your points, make your points lessons to learn. Put a verb in every point. Help your students become "doers of the Word." Keep your lesson simple and it will be memorable.

QUESTION #7: WHAT IS THE MOST POWERFUL WAY TO SAY IT?

After determining the most simple, encouraging, and positive way to relay God's Word, then determine the most powerful way to relay it. The personal way to relate the truths of God's Word is the most powerful way. No presentation is more effective than a personal testimony. Paul knew it. "We loved you so much that we were delighted to share with you not only the gospel of God but our lives as well" (1 Thessalonians 2:8).

A person with a testimony is more persuasive than a person with an argument. You will be far more effective as a witness than you can ever be as an orator. How do you share in the most personal and powerful way?

1. Share your struggles and weaknesses. Do not be afraid to be transparent. Note Paul's example: "I think you ought to know, dear brothers, about the hard time we went through in Asia. We were really crushed and overwhelmed, and

feared we would never live through it" (2 Corinthians 1:8, *The Living Bible*). Confessional teaching creates credibility. The real secret of effective communication is the ability to drop your mask and share your deeply felt emotions. Although you may be misunderstood by a few, you will emotionally connect with many. For example, when teaching on anger, share about a time when you had difficulty controlling your temper.

2. Share where you are making progress. People grow best when they have a model to follow. You cannot mold without modeling. Paul said, "Follow me as I follow Christ" (see 1 Corinthians 11:1, author's paraphrase). Jesus demonstrated this incarnational type of teaching. The minister is the message. You must model your message. You must seek to grow in the same areas you are challenging your students to grow in.

3. Share what you are currently learning. Paul says our very lives were further proof of the truth of the message: "Our gospel came to you with deep conviction" (author's paraphrase; see 1 Corinthians 2:1–5; 1 Thessalonians 1:5). Throughout history, the people who have changed the world have not been necessarily the smartest, the most educated, the most intelligent, or the wealthiest. The people who have changed the world, for better or for worse, have been the people with the deepest convictions. Pass on to your students the insights that God is teaching you right now. Influence is caused by personal conviction. In all probability, what is affecting you will also affect your students.

QUESTION #8: WHAT IS THE MOST EFFECTIVE WAY TO SAY IT?

Many different methods can be used to communicate a truth. Wise teachers vary their methods from week to week. During the course of a lesson, a teacher can employ a variety of methods—lecture, storytelling, discussion, questions and answers, visual aids, drama—to help the pacing of the class.

Don't be afraid to try a method you have never used before. It may improve your teaching and make your class fun!

The Purpose of Teaching for Maturity

The preceding pages of this chapter have dealt with the process of teaching. Many teachers' training manuals stop at this point. However, the process is not the most important aspect of teaching. If the goal of teaching is changed lives and transformed characters, then the test of teaching is, very simply, are changed lives being produced? The ultimate goal for the teacher who has maturity as a goal is to equip the saints for ministry. In Ephesians 4:11–16, Paul assigns the pastors and teachers a role in the body of Christ: the perfecting, or equipping, of the saints to do the work of the ministry. The most effective teachers equip believers to become equippers. Every member is to serve as a minister!

The church modeled after Ephesians 4 is exciting! Imagine a church in which every member had a ministry. The church would be a center of energy and activity. Everyone would have a part in the growth process. From the youngest child to the most senior adult, each part of the church body would serve a purpose to enhance the Body as a whole. Who would not want to be a part of a church like that?

To accomplish this objective, the goal of equipping the saints for ministry, we have to rethink our traditional approach to teacher training.

The typical Sunday school teacher's job description looks something like this:

- Arrive at least 30 minutes early for your class each week, so you are able to greet newcomers and visitors.
- Thoroughly prepare your assigned lesson each week.
- Prepare all handouts, work sheets, etc., prior to the class session.
- Contact every class absentee and visitor by phone or mail each week.

- Inform the superintendent at least 1 week in advance of any Sunday that you will be absent.
- Upon conclusion of the class period, be sure the room is straightened and all materials returned to their proper place.
- Pray for your students on a regular basis.
- Be consistent in church attendance as an example for your students.

Every one of these items is very important. We need to be prepared, thorough, and attentive to detail. However, God's job description for teachers may be quite different. In *The 7 Laws of the Learner*, Bruce Wilkinson presents God's Job Description for All Teachers based on Ephesians 4:16. Then he asks, "What then is the Lord going to be looking for when He evaluates us as teachers."

Consider some startling core issues that God has revealed will probably be on our final exam:

1. The nature of the ministry that our students are involved in ("work of ministry"). We tend to have a completely different mind-set than God about our teaching. His emphasis is always on what our students do; our emphasis is upon what we, the teachers, do. His emphasis is upon the work of ministry our students are engaged in; our emphasis is upon the course outline and notes we are engaged in. The first question God may ask us will likely focus upon the specific work of ministry that our students are doing as a result of our class.

2. The percentage of our class who are personally ministering ("every part"). Notice again the contrast in mind-set. God's emphasis is always upon the full participation of all members; our emphasis is upon the 20 percent who seem to be "faithful." Somehow we have compromised and allowed 80 percent nonparticipation. God's standard is "every part," and, therefore, we will be evaluated on that basis.

3. The degree to which our students are doing the work of the ministry according to their capacity ("its share"). What a striking mind-set the Lord presents in this and other key New Testament passages—that He has given to each believer not only a unique personality but also sovereignly bestowed a spiritual gift for the purpose of ministry. All too often we think that as long as a person is "doing something for God," we have accomplished our duty and fulfilled our commission. The Lord is not looking for us to settle for 10-talent people doing 2-talent works of service! Nor is He pleased when His children are misplaced outside the area in which He has sovereignly gifted them.

4. The quality and quantity of the work done by our students ("effective working"). When God finished His work of creation, He stepped back and evaluated it and exclaimed, "It is good!" God is a God of excellence and all His works are excellent. He expects us, as commissioned officers in His teaching army, to continually train and upgrade the performance of our students. Too few classes have an objective standard of performance beyond some testing of the content. Not only is the Lord concerned that our students are working, but He is concerned that they are effectively working. To have effective workers, we must be effective teachers.

5. The percentage of growth in our class ("cause growth of the body"). Whenever we take the Lord at His word and do His work in His way, we can be sure to see the results He has promised. As people actively use their spiritual gifts in effective ministry, the Lord promises it will "cause growth of the body." Such a class cannot help but grow! Unlike God's mind-set and promises, however, our mind-set is that effective teaching will not necessarily result in class growth. Ephesians says effective teaching "causes growth of the body," which should not be limited to merely spiritual growth. For a biblical model, note the explosive growth of the church in the early chapters of Acts.

6. Constant, normal, and spontaneous mutual ministry between class members ("edify itself in love"). The mind-set of most teachers is that they are the ones almost single-handedly responsible to minister to their students. In contrast, the Lord expects our students to minister to each other as if they were the teacher or minister. God is concerned that Christians not just meet together, but actually meet so that mutual edification takes place. He desires each member of His church to become more and more self-initiating so that when they see or hear of any need, they immediately respond out of a sense of ownership and responsibility.[27]

Wow! There is a great difference between our criteria for success and God's criteria for success. The mind-set of the typical teacher is far different from God's expectation. We focus on our teaching, what we do. God focuses on our students, what they become. Imagine the difference if teachers were to set out to accomplish God's objectives for their classes! Here are just a few of the differences:

- The *attention* would be directed to the response of the students, rather than the talent of the teacher.
- The *evaluation* would center upon the student's growth in ministry, rather than the teacher's performance of specified tasks.
- The *responsibility* for caring for the class would be transferred from the teacher to all members of the Body.
- The *ministry* of the class would be expanded as all members did their share.

In most local church settings, the primary forum for discipleship is the Sunday school class. To produce mature believers, we must intentionally teach for maturity. This intentional maturing requires attention to the process of teaching but also requires careful attention to the product of teaching. Many teachers are content with mastering the proper process, never evaluating the product. We must do all!

The Product of Teaching for Maturity

The product of teaching for maturity is members that are becoming actively engaged in service and ministry. Teaching for maturity will create growth in your class and growth in your church. As more people are placed into ministry service, the ministry potential of the church grows, allowing it to minister to greater numbers of people. Equipping the saints for service and launching them in ministry begins a cycle of growth and excitement. New ministries will be started and new segments of the community will be reached.

Churches that have adopted this lay ministry model have found that equipping the person in the pew for service results in creativity in ministry like they never imagined. As church members seek to find their place of service, God leads them to innovative ideas for ministry. Consider just some of the unconventional ministries that have been started by equipped saints:

- A retired senior citizen started a food and clothing pantry to minister to the homeless of his community.
- A young man in his 20s began a ministry to skateboarders. Soon, hundreds of teenagers were hearing the gospel each week.
- A plumber in his 50s felt called to minister in the prison system of his state. He currently leads numerous inmates in Bible studies every week.
- A homemaker began a ministry to young mothers, who meet together for fellowship, instruction, prayer, and support.
- A businessman who took early retirement assumes the ministry of "pastoral care." He cares for his pastors, praying for them and helping them with various tasks.
- A single woman who survived an abusive marriage begins a weekly outreach to a women's shelter.

How can these types of ministries begin in your church? Equip every believer for service. The product of teaching for maturity is exciting, innovative, explosive ministry!

2
Base

6
The Corporate
Maturity

Attitudes

Maturity should not only be an outgrowth of Sunday school classes and small groups, but should be an outgrowth of every aspect of the church. The disciple-making church focuses on the goal of maturity in every age-group and in every area. Each member of your class should grow in every area of church life.

Developing the right attitudes is an important component of growth and maturity. Often the only difference between growth and stagnancy is attitude. To receive maximum benefit from class, small groups, and corporate worship services, the growing believer must have the right attitude.

We should seek to reproduce four attitudes in our disciples.

AN ATTITUDE OF EXPECTANCY

We attend church often. Many people attend Sunday morning service, Sunday school, Sunday night service, and Wednesday night service. It is easy to show up and go through the motions, just carrying out a routine. Church is special! It is a wonderful privilege to worship in God's presence. But sometimes we sing in the song service, pray for requests, and sit through a sermon, all without showing any interest. Why? Because we come to church without expectancy.

People with an attitude of expectancy are ready to receive something from God every time they come to church, Sunday school, or open their Bibles in personal devotions. Expectancy prompts students to listen intently, take notes, and respond to challenges! You can expect to receive something from God every time His Word is opened. The person who lacks expectancy wonders, Why wasn't I ministered to today? This person complains about not "being fed." Such people are not fed because they are not expecting food. They are not looking to grow. The Book of Acts tells the wonderful story of a man who had an attitude of expectancy.

One day Peter and John were going up to the temple at the time of prayer—at three in the afternoon. Now a man crippled from birth was being carried to the temple gate called Beautiful, where he was put every day to beg from those going into the temple courts. When he saw Peter and John about to enter, he asked them for money. Peter looked straight at him, as did John. Then Peter said, "Look at us!" So the man gave them his attention, *expecting to get something* from them. Then Peter said, "Silver or gold I do not have, but what I have I give you. In the name of Jesus Christ of Nazareth, walk." Taking him by the right hand, he helped him up, and instantly the man's feet and ankles became strong. He jumped to his feet and began to walk. Then he went with them into the temple courts, walking and jumping, and praising God. When all the people saw him walking and praising God, they recognized him as the same man who used to sit begging at the temple gate called Beautiful, and they were filled with wonder and amazement at what had happened to him (Acts 3:1–10, emphasis added).

The man was expecting to get something *before* he knew what he might receive. His expectancy led to his miracle. When you enter the church, expect to receive something from God!

When the pastor begins the sermon, expect to learn something from God's Word. When we expect to receive, we receive.

AN ATTITUDE OF TOLERANCE

In the typical church sanctuary, what holds up the roof? There is a large area of floor space with no columns and no visible support for the roof area. What keeps it from crashing down on the heads of the congregation? What makes it stay in the air, seemingly on its own accord? The answer is tension. Tension keeps the roof in the air. The roof is composed of many beams and cross-members pulling in opposite directions. The tension between them holds your roof together.

How does this apply to a church? Diversity can create tension. The only groups who will not tolerate diversity are cults. Many people only want to fellowship and worship with people who are like themselves. They are unwilling to allow people with different tastes, preferences, or styles to become a part of the group. Churches, classes, and groups will never grow if they adopt an "us four and no more" attitude. The possibility exists that you may have already reached everyone who is exactly like you. To build a great church, we must recognize the value God places on each individual. We cannot reject a single person that Christ died for.

AN ATTITUDE OF COMMUNITY

An attitude of community is important in every church and class. This attitude has to do with our fellowship, our love for each other. Jesus indicated this attitude is the standard by which others will judge our discipleship. "A new command I give you: Love one another. As I have loved you, so you must love one another. By this all men will know that you are my disciples, if you love one another" (John 13:34,35). The church of the 21st century will be challenged to demonstrate love in an increasingly hateful and hurtful world. Our visible love for each other and the world will identify us as the church of

Jesus Christ. Our love for each other will allow us to overcome differences of opinion and controversial issues. "Most important of all, continue to show deep love for each other, for love makes up for many of your faults" (1 Peter 4:8, *The Living Bible*).

AN ATTITUDE OF SERVICE

The mature believer will develop an attitude of service, often referred to as a "servant's heart." A believer with this attitude will willingly put others before self and will serve the church with a joyful spirit. A servant's heart allows you to view every task, chore, or assignment as a ministry. This attitude is a key to maturity. Jesus exemplified the quality of servant leadership. Philippians 2:5 says, "Your attitude should be the same as that of Christ Jesus." Rather than coming to earth with a royal retinue, He came alone to a humble manger. He gave up His life for our sin, illustrating the ultimate attitude of sacrifice.

> I am the good shepherd; I know my sheep and my sheep know me—just as the Father knows me and I know the Father—and I lay down my life for the sheep. I have other sheep that are not of this sheep pen. I must bring them also. They too will listen to my voice, and there shall be one flock and one shepherd. The reason my Father loves me is that I lay down my life—only to take it up again. No one takes it from me, but I lay it down of my own accord (John 10:14–18).

In the same way, we serve Him by giving our lives, our talents, and our abilities.

Habits

There are many habits that can be developed and methods that can be utilized in a church that will help to promote maturity in the lives of individual members.

NOTE TAKING

> Psychologists tell us we have the potential of remembering only
> up to 10 percent of what we hear. And that's potential, not actual.
> As a matter of fact, if you do remember 10 percent of what you
> hear, you're in the genius category. Unfortunately, the bulk of
> Christian education is hearing-oriented. That's why it's often so
> inefficient. If we add seeing to hearing, psychologists say our
> potential for remembering goes up to 50 percent. That's why visu-
> al aids are so important. We live in a visually oriented society.[28]

We want people to remember what we teach! Our teaching
will not result in maturity if it is quickly forgotten. One very
effective method to allow people to see and hear the information being taught is to provide outlines, allowing the listeners
to fill in the appropriate blanks. In many churches, sermon
notes are provided in the bulletin, and teachers provide outlines in each class. Members can then maintain a journal in
which they compile all of their sermon and class notes.

REPETITION

Consider our earliest stages of development. We learn to
walk by attempting steps over and over. We learn to talk by
hearing our parents endlessly repeat mama and dada. Repetition is a very effective method of learning! As teachers we
cannot be afraid to repeat information and applications until
they are reproduced in the lives of our students. Jesus modeled
this style of learning. He taught His disciples the importance of
a servant's heart on several different occasions. Jesus washed
their feet (John 13:5). He told them, "I tell you the truth, no servant is greater than his master, nor is a messenger greater
than the one who sent him" (John 13:16). On an-other occasion
Jesus answered His disciples, saying, "Not so with you. Instead,
whoever wants to become great among you must be your servant, and whoever wants to be first must be your slave" (Matthew 20:26,27). Jesus reinforced the truth through repetition.

American author and editor Clifton Fadiman once said, "When you reread a classic you do not see more in the book than you did before; you see more in *you* than was there before." That adage is even truer when studying the Bible. Each time we repeat a truth, it becomes further in-grained in our lives.

AUDIOVISUAL AIDS

Our memory is increased when we see the information. Many different visual aids can be utilized to increase comprehension. Sermon or lesson points can be displayed on a screen using video projectors or conventional overheads. Points can be illustrated with a short video clip or a skit performed by class members. Using a variety of methods and media helps to make a message memorable. This is effective at all age levels. When teaching children, you can use video, crafts, clay, coloring papers, puppets, or songs to reinforce the central theme. When teaching youth, you can use video, current articles from magazines and newspapers, drama, and music videos to help illustrate your message.

APPLICATION ASSIGNMENTS AND PARALLEL READING

Students are more likely to assimilate information and apply it to their lives if the information is reinforced outside the classroom. A teacher can increase the effectiveness of the message by assigning parallel reading or application exercises. Reading *My Utmost for His Highest* by Oswald Chambers can strengthen a teaching on personal devotions and quiet time. A message on parenting can be supplemented by reading *The Strong-Willed Child* by James Dobson. A pastor or teacher can assign books that will provide further insight and knowledge on a topic.

Application exercises are powerful tools to integrate teaching into life habits. After teaching on soul winning, a teacher may instruct each student to share the faith with one individual. After a lesson on forgiveness, each student can write a letter to an offender offering forgiveness. A teacher who is seeking to produce maturity will often assign an action to follow up on the learning. If adding seeing to hearing increases learning, how much more is it increased by adding doing?

> Psychologists say this combination brings the percentage of memory to 90 percent.... I learned early on that students can memorize materials in any way you ask them to and on an exam they can tell you it all. You can give them a great big A for it. Brilliant. Yet give them the same examination 3 days later and they couldn't pass it if their life depended on it. But after getting students involved in the process, I've tested them 25 years later and they still know and are using the same Bible-study principles they learned in my class—and which they never memorized. They learned by usage. They learned in the process of activity. The same is true in other aspects of the Christian life.... Get involved in the process. That's the best way to learn anything.[29]

Why Believers Do Not Grow

Many church members know the right thing to do. They have been properly taught the habits and attitudes of a mature believer. Yet some believers do not grow. Why? What keeps these people from growing? Many Christians are not growing because they are not doing what they know to do. They are armed with the correct information but for some reason do not act on that information. Every teacher has encountered the faithful student who soaks up knowledge but resists life change. This type of individual is a source of great frustration! To help such students grow, we must first understand why they are not growing.

Most people who fail in their dreams fail not from a lack of ability but from a lack of commitment. It is one thing to know what to do, but another thing entirely to do what you know. It is easier to blame God, the devil, or others for our failures than to accept the fact that our situations are most often the direct result of our own decisions. "A person's own foolishness ruins his life, but in his mind he blames the LORD" (Proverbs 19:3, NCV).

The good news is this: Most of the things in our lives that can help us succeed will be determined by our choices. The bad news is this: Most people fail to make the right choices. Several things keep people from making the choice to do what they know to do.

FALTER IN COMMITMENT

John Maxwell says:

> Until I am committed, there is a hesitancy, a chance to draw back. But the moment I definitely commit myself, God moves also, and a whole stream of events erupt. All manner of unforeseen incidents, meetings, persons, and material assistance which I could never have dreamed would come my way begin to flow toward me—the moment I make a commitment.

In the area of commitment, you can ask yourself these five questions:

1. What do I really desire?
2. What will it take for it to happen?
3. Does it matter enough that I will do whatever is necessary to see it occur?
4. Have I delayed beginning?
5. Who can help me get there?

J. C. Penney once said, "Unless you are willing to drench yourself in your work beyond the capacity of the average man, you are just not cut out for positions at the top." To go beyond the average position, you have to do more than the average person. In *The One-Minute Manager* Ken Blanchard says, "There's a difference between interest and commitment. When you are interested in doing something, you do it only when it is convenient. When you are committed to something, you accept no excuses." Many people do not act on the correct information they possess because they are unwilling to make a commitment.

FEAR OF FAILURE

It is hard to believe, but successful people experience failure almost as often as unsuccessful people. On the average, successful people fail two times out of every five times they attempt something, and unsuccessful people fail three times out of every five times. Everyone fails. There is not one person who does not experience failure. Some people do not do what is right because they fear failure.

Not only does everyone fail, but we all fail often. Too many people when they fail erect a monument to their failure and spend the rest of their lives paying homage. Some people dwell on a single failure for years! We should view failure as a moment, a fleeting experience. Charles Kettering said, "Virtually nothing comes out right the first time. Repeated failures are fingerposts on the road to achievement. The only time that you don't fail is the last time you try something and it works. One fails forward." For many people, their fear of failing is so acute that they never even start. At the turn of the twentieth century Elbert Hubbard said, "There is no failure except in no longer trying."

Nothing is ever attempted without some obstacles. Failure does not have to be defeat. Starting is the first step to succeeding. For people to act on the information they receive, they must develop the courage to begin.

FIGHT CHANGE

The world is continually changing. In recent years the policy of planned obsolescence has been adopted by manufacturing. Planned obsolescence means the life span of a product is predetermined, built-in. Computers are put together with the knowledge that new technology will make them obsolete in 3 years. Cars are manufactured with the knowledge that they will last only so long. If you are between 18 and 21 years old, over half the nations on earth were not existing in their present form when you were born. Average Americans born in the 90s will hold 8 different jobs and live in 30 different homes during their lives! We live in a world of continual change!

Very few people enjoy change. In fact, the only person who always enjoys change is a wet baby. You may be saying, "I don't resist change." If you think you like change, try this simple test: Tonight when you sit down to dinner with your family, let someone else sit in your seat. We are creatures of habit! In some churches, people will refuse to stay for service if someone else is seated in their pew!

People resist change for several reasons:

- Misunderstanding. When the purpose of change is not made clear, it causes anxiety and fear.
- Lack of ownership. People resist change when they feel left out of the process.
- Habit patterns. It is difficult to change habits developed over the course of time.
- Insufficient reward. When the pain in change is greater than in remaining the same, no change will occur.
- Threatened by loss. When people are threatened with the loss of something they deem valuable—money, security, control—they resist change.
- Tradition. It is difficult to accept a new thing when "we have always done it this way."
- Personal criticism. Some people resist change because they are afraid they will be criticized if they change.

When will people change? John Maxwell teaches that people will change when they hurt enough they have to, when they learn enough they want to, or when they receive enough power that they are able to.

FAVOR "THAT WILL DO" AS THEIR MOTTO

People often do not grow because they adopt an attitude of just getting by. You hear them use statements such as "That's good enough." "Good enough for government work." "It will do." "Nobody will ever know the difference." "Well, it's not perfect, but it will work." Successful people always give more than they expect to get. They don't settle for mediocrity. James Francis Burns, secretary of state to Franklin Roosevelt, said,

> I discovered at an early age that most of the differences between average people and great people can be explained in three words—"and then some." Top people do what is expected of them—and then some. They are considerate and thoughtful of others—and then some. They meet their obligations and responsibilities—and then some.

The "and then some" attitude enables us to continue to do what is right when others are giving up.

FAULTY PERCEPTION

People fail to do what they know is correct when their perception is faulty. When we have a faulty perception, we often fail to see the bigger picture of what God is doing in our lives. We confuse our perception of good with the ultimate good. People make decisions based upon short-term satisfaction instead of long-term growth. We rarely see our faults, our weaknesses, or our flaws as God sees them. When people lack discernment, they often see things incorrectly.

FALL INTO INCONSISTENT BEHAVIOR

Consistency is a mark of maturity. Fads and emotions may come and go, but people who can be consistent will be successful in putting their knowledge into practice. Proverbs speaks of the consistent man: "Most men will proclaim every one his own goodness: but a faithful man who can find?" (Proverbs 20:6, KJV).

The opposite of the consistent person is the convenience person. Consider the following differences between convenience and consistent people:

- Convenience people are emotion based; consistent people are character based.
- Convenience people do what is easiest; consistent people do what is right.
- Convenience people are controlled by their moods; consistent people are controlled by their priorities.
- Convenience people have a selfish mind-set; consistent people have a servant mind-set.
- Convenience people look for excuses; consistent people look for solutions.
- Convenience people quit during tough times; consistent people continue in tough times.[30]

People often fail to do what they know is right, as they become inconsistent.

FAIL IN RELATIONSHIPS

Success is 13 percent product knowledge and 87 percent people knowledge. Many people do not do what they should because they fail in relationships with others. John Maxwell, speaking about relationships, says, "When people do not like you, if they can they will hurt you. If they cannot hurt you, they will not help you. If they have to help you, they will not hope for you. If they will not hope for you, even if you achieve, the victory is hollow." If you cannot get along with other people, it is difficult to put knowledge of maturity into practice. To the mature believer, relationships are more important than accomplishments.

7
Creating
Programs for
Maturity

Every church should have the goal of producing disciples. However, often the difficulty comes in coordinating each department and class to ensure that the maturation process is continuing in every area. It is essential that every age-group, department, specialized ministry, leader, worker, and staff member understand and work toward the common goal. For the local body of Christ to function properly, each part must understand its purpose in the overall mission. The apostle Paul illustrated this synergistic relationship in a familiar passage:

Now the body is not made up of one part but of many. If the foot should say, "Because I am not a hand, I do not belong to the body," it would not for that reason cease to be part of the body. And if the ear should say, "Because I am not an eye, I do not belong to the body," it would not for that reason cease to be part of the body. If the whole body were an eye, where would the sense of hearing be? If the whole body were an ear, where would the sense of smell be? But in fact God has arranged the parts in the body, every one of them, just as he wanted them to be. If they were all one part, where would the body be? As it is, there are many parts, but one body (1 Corinthians 12:14–20).

We need people involved in every ministry. The healthy church has individuals of varying talents, gifts, and personalities serving in ministries that suit their strengths.

At First Assembly of God in North Little Rock, Arkansas, over 600 laypeople take part in a variety of ministries: Sunday school, Royal Rangers, Missionettes, sidewalk Sunday school, children's church, nursery, parking lot ministry, security, ushers, greeters, hospitality, library, sound, lights, media, television, choir, orchestra, meal preparation, preschool, maintenance, prison outreaches, and many others. Such a large number of volunteers require that various components be in place to ensure a unified direction. At First Assembly, every ministry is guided by the mission statement of the church, which includes the phrase "to disciple believers." It is a vital part of the church's strategy to produce maturity in its members. How then do you coordinate, evaluate, and create ministries to produce maturity? How do we ensure that every part of the Body is fulfilling its purpose for the ultimate good of the church and the kingdom of God, that every program is focused toward the common goal of producing mature believers? By employing eight components.

Component #1: Establish Clear Objectives and Expectations

Often ministries are not focused on a common goal simply because it isn't clearly stated. Each ministry leader must have a clearly defined set of objectives and expectations in order to set the stage for future evaluation. Evaluation is difficult without having established a criteria. How can we hold someone responsible for not producing disciples if we never told them they were supposed to? For example, at First Assembly, a discipleship group leader of men's ministry has the following expectations and objectives:

- Pray for every man in your group every week.
- Contact each member of your group every week.

- Study and complete everything you require your group members to study and complete.
- Complete the assigned course of study in 14 weeks.
- At the conclusion of your 14-week study, be prepared to identify at least one man in your group who has grown to the place where he can now lead a group.
- Be open, honest, and transparent with your group.
- Share your struggles with the group and illustrate God's help in overcoming the difficulties.
- In addition to preparing a weekly session, spend a minimum of 30 minutes each day in Bible study and prayer.
- Be committed to faithful church attendance, including Sunday morning, Sunday night, and Wednesday night.
- Pray with your group members at the altar.

Each man desiring to lead a group was given these expectations before being assigned a group. Some, when seeing the expectations, may choose not to lead. But leaders who understand what is required are better equipped to meet the demands of the vision.

Component #2: Buy in to the Vision

At First Assembly, in order to work in any area, you must first believe in "the vision of the house." The children of Israel learned this important principle while in the wilderness. Moses became frustrated because of the complaints of the people. They were tired of manna. Moses prayed, telling God that the burden of leading the people and responding to their every need was becoming more than he could bear. God responded to Moses:

Bring me seventy of Israel's elders who are known to you as leaders and officials among the people. Have them come to the Tent of Meeting, that they may stand there with you. I will come down and speak with you there, and I will take of the Spirit that is on you and put the Spirit on them. They will help you carry the burden of the people so that you will not have to carry it alone (Numbers 11:16,17).

Later in the chapter we read that God did what He promised; He anointed leaders to assist Moses:

So Moses went out and told the people what the Lord had said. He brought together seventy of their elders and had them stand around the Tent. Then the Lord came down in the cloud and spoke with him, and he took of the Spirit that was on him and put the Spirit on the seventy elders (Numbers 11:24,25).

The leaders of Israel were given the vision of their leader. If staff members, lay leaders, and volunteers do not have the vision of the leader, they will not be able to work effectively in the church. People must have the spirit of the leader if they are going to lead in the common direction. The elders of Israel could not bear the burden of the people until they had the spirit of the leader—Moses. When people catch the spirit and the vision that God has placed upon their leader, they can flow in a common anointing in accomplishing the goal.

When the Apostles laid hands on the deacons, Philip and Stephen went out and worked miracles, signs, and wonders. Why? They had the same Spirit on them as the Apostles. They weren't apostles, but they possessed the Spirit. Many individuals in churches are filled with the Holy Spirit—operating in gifts and possessing a clear anointing—but have never gotten in tune with "the vision of the house." They are Christians, they are in the house, but they have yet to buy in to the vision. Jesus said, "A house divided cannot stand"(see Matthew 12:25, author's paraphrase). If you have two visions in the house, you have division.

So at First Assembly, before people are placed into ministry, they must first determine if they are in agreement with the vision and the goal of producing disciples. Our mission statement is expanded to include these eight statements that ministry leaders should agree with.

EVANGELISM MUST TAKE PRIORITY OVER EVENTS

The church in the 90s seems addicted to events: illustrated sermons, musical extravaganzas, fireworks celebrations, big-name guests, concerts, dramas, pageants. Many churches have become event driven, living for the next big day. We have determined that evangelism is our priority. As a church we miss some large crowds and wonderful publicity by refusing to host any event or have any guest that does not fit the vision of the church. Nevertheless, very event must meet the criteria of leading people to Jesus.

THE BIG PICTURE TAKES PRIORITY OVER PROGRAMS

We strive to be a "big picture" church. Our interest is not in having the most programs, the best brochures, or the latest ministry fad. In fact, we have fewer programs than most churches our size. The big picture of First Assembly is our common goal, our mission. We aim to move people along a continuum from salvation to sanctification to ultimate glorification. Some programs do not fit our picture. When we see the big picture, it eliminates the narrow focus of individual efforts.

ANOINTING TAKES PRIORITY OVER ABILITY

Talent and ability are great. In many churches, leaders are selected solely on the criteria of talent. We want our most talented people serving in the area of their gifts. But nothing is more powerful than a talented person operating in the presence of a Holy anointing. Some talented people we choose not to use. Why? Their priority is on their talent, the performance. A God-anointed monotone is more effective than a professional voice without God's power. A less than skilled teacher can be powerfully effective when anointed by God's Holy Spirit.

ACCOUNTABILITY TAKES PRIORITY OVER AUTHORITY

Scripture teaches that everything God does is accomplished on the basis of His authority. Scripture also teaches that God delegates authority to the church, civil government, and family. We believe strongly in the purpose of authority but recognize the balance of accountability. Every leader is accountable to the vision, mission, and leadership of the church.

MATURITY TAKES PRIORITY OVER MINISTRY

It is wonderful to minister. In fact, it is everyone's responsibility to be a minister of reconciliation. But that ministry must flow out of maturity. Maturity results from teaching, discipleship training, and accountability. Ministers must first take upon themselves the responsibility of becoming mature. This is vital! It is impossible to produce mature believers if the leadership team is composed of immature members!

UNITY TAKES PRIORITY OVER UNIFORMITY

Uniformity is outside pressure based on compulsion. Unity is inside pressure based on compassion. We not only tolerate but encourage diversity. In fact, one of our greatest strengths lies in our diversity. In the continually changing climate of society, we must recognize the difference between substance and style, between principle and preference. Many churches miss valuable opportunities for ministry due to an imbalanced emphasis on style. We seek to tolerate differences in style but never at the expense of substance. Our content must remain constant. Cults are the only groups who will not tolerate diversity.

CORPORATE CONVICTION TAKES PRIORITY OVER CONGREGATIONAL COMFORT

It is currently popular to embrace church growth models based on Baby-Boomer statistics. This model seeks to establish a comfort level acceptable to every attender. However, the nature of the gospel is confrontational. Jesus confronted sin; we must confront sin. We can always close the backdoor of the church by compromise. But without conviction, our Pentecostal distinctives lose preeminence.

PASTORAL CARE TAKES PRIORITY OVER PERSONAL CONVENIENCE

Pastoral care does not come only from the paid pastoral team. All teachers are pastoral-care ministers and responsible for care. At First Assembly, we are looking for "second milers" to serve on our team. Ministry personnel are not allowed to make statements such as "It's not in my job description" or "I have my rights." Those statements and their corresponding attitudes have no place on the leadership team. The nature of care is such that it is rarely convenient. Mature leaders are willing to give up their personal convenience in order to minister to others.

Every church must have a vision! Each member of the ministry team should understand the vision and be committed to functioning to achieve its goal.

Component #3: Evaluate Every Program Annually

Many churches launch programs with great care and high expectations. However, no program that is left unevaluated will maintain a high performance. Over time, particularly during changes in leadership, programs started with the best intentions can often drift. To ensure that every ministry in the church is reaching the goal of producing mature believers, we can ask ten questions.

1. What was the original purpose of the ministry?
2. Is the ministry fulfilling its original purpose?
3. Has the purpose changed or been added to?
4. Is the purpose still important to the organization?
5. Is there a better way to accomplish the same purpose?
6. Who is being ministered to?
7. Are people growing as a result of the ministry?
8. Is the ministry and its leadership in line with the vision and current direction of the church?
9. Is the ministry producing new leaders?
10. If we were to cancel this ministry today, what would be the result?

All too often, evaluation is reserved until a crisis. If every ministry is evaluated every year, problems can be arrested before they become crises. Each year every ministry, class, and department should be evaluated. This evaluation helps to ensure that the common direction of the church is kept in focus. Consider this recent evaluation of the Sunday school program at a large Assemblies of God church:

1. What was the original purpose of the ministry? This church is an 80-year-old church that has always emphasized Sunday school. The original purpose of Sunday school was twofold: evangelism and discipleship.

2. Is the ministry fulfilling its original purpose? Currently, yes. New members continue to be added to the church as the result of outreach efforts of Sunday school classes. Christian training is occurring at all age levels, with carefully selected growth opportunities for believers at all stages of Christian development.

3. Has the purpose changed or been added to? Yes. Sunday school also fulfills the need for small group ministry. We choose to use Sunday school as our primary vehicle for small group interaction, fellowship, and bonding. Groups meet as an extension of the various adult classes. Sunday school also serves as the front line of pastoral care. Teachers, leaders, and visitation personnel are often the first persons on the scene in a crisis.

4. Is the purpose still important to the organization? Yes. Sunday school is currently the single most effective method for discipleship training and small group ministry. Sunday school is the most effective way of assimilating new people into the church body.

5. Is there a better way to accomplish the same purpose? No. To replace Sunday school would require beginning at least three new ministries. Sunday school remains a viable, thriving ministry.

6. Who is being ministered to? Sunday school attendance fig-

ures are 80 percent of morning worship attendance figures. Four out of five families are involved in Sunday school.

7. Are people growing as a result of the ministry? Yes. Individuals can be identified who are moving through the growth process and being launched into ministry. Classes are growing numerically and spiritually.

8. Are the ministry and its leadership in line with the vision and current direction of the church? Yes. Sunday school continues to thrive in accordance with the vision of the corporate body. However, there are a few areas where leadership changes will enhance our ability to further thecorporate vision. These areas have been identified and will be addressed in this calendar year.

9. Is the ministry producing new leaders? Yes. In the past year, class members have become Sunday school teachers, children's church leaders, sidewalk Sunday school workers, and various other ministry leaders. In addition, two new classes have been started utilizing new teachers discipled by others.

10. If we were to cancel this ministry today, what would be the result? Canceling Sunday school would result in a large hole in our overall strategy. We would have to institute a small group ministry program. In addition, many members would lose their place of ministry.

This evaluation helped the church in determining that Sunday school not only was healthy and growing but needed additional emphasis. Sunday school was fulfilling both of its original purposes and had grown to address many other vital needs.

Component #4: Evaluate
the Current Growth of Members

Not only must programs be evaluated but also the membership, that is, its growth and development. It is important to know what percentage of people are tithing, serving in ministry, or participating in growth opportunities. Evaluating the membership as a whole is often difficult. One method of evaluation is the survey: of a congregation, department, or class. On a periodic basis, time can be taken in a Sunday morning service or class to distribute a survey to every member. That information allows examination of the demographics, behaviors, and habits of the person in the pew.

From a recent survey, one church learned the following information about their constituency.

- Baby Busters and their families make up 13 percent of the church.
- Baby Boomers and their families, 43 percent of the church.
- Builders and their families, 44 percent of the church.
- Over 83 percent of attenders were referred by a friend, family member, or minister.
- Approximately 7 percent of attenders first came because of advertising.
- Over 70 percent continue to attend the church because of the preaching, just over 20 percent because of departmental ministries, and 9 percent because of the music or worship.
- Sixty-eight percent regularly tithe.
- Almost 40 percent are in a ministry position.
- Forty-five percent have been attending the church 5 years or less.
- Between 42 percent and 43 percent of attenders had no Pentecostal background.

After compiling the results of the survey, the church designed programs and implemented strategies to strengthen the weaknesses. A new class was started to introduce people of varying backgrounds to the doctrinal distinctives of Pentecost. A sermon series on stewardship was preached, to address the 32 percent that were not currently tithing. A Wednesday night series was taught on ministry gifts in which each person filled out a gift-evaluation test. Ministry positions were evaluated and expanded to allow more people the opportunity to serve. A Sunday school class was designed for parents of the Baby Buster era, improving efforts to reach the 30 and under age-group.

Know the numbers in your church or class—the *real numbers*! Count heads, keep records, maintain an average; but determine what you have. Knowing where you are now is vital to determining where you need to be in the future.

Component #5: Be Willing to Stop Ineffective Ministries

To continue to produce maturity in accordance with the vision, we must be willing to stop ineffective ministries. Churches are saddled with programs that were once vibrant and healthy but have grown tiresome and stale. We have to stop what is not working! It is not enough to merely evaluate. We must act on the results of our evaluation. If the ministry is not meeting the vision of the church, if it is not in agreement with the mission statement, if it is not actively involved in producing disciples, it may be time to pull the plug. An unwillingness to discontinue a ministry results in valuable volunteers, rooms, finances, and promotional efforts being consumed by a mediocre project.

Every ministry, when first begun, should have a trial period. This is called "setting a sunset." Rather than announcing, "We are now going to have a Sunday school class for the deaf," announce, "For the next 6 months, we are offering a class for the deaf. We will reevaluate it in January." In this example, a class for the deaf is a good thing. But what if no deaf people come? Will we continue the class because it was a "good idea" or because "it would be horrible to say we no longer have a deaf ministry"? Many churches continue with programs that have no discernible purpose. In fact, even the leaders of the ministry don't often know why it exists, and the familiar defense "we've always done it that way" echoes through the empty room.

Component #6: Model Maturity in Leadership

Besides being willing to stop ineffective programs, we must also be willing to replace ineffective leaders. To produce mature believers, disciples, the leadership must model maturity. A familiar leadership maxim says it rather succinctly: You teach what you know; you reproduce what you are. Immature leaders will produce immature followers. At First Assembly, the following questions are often asked of the leadership team:

- If everyone attended like you attend, what kind of stability would we have?
- If everyone gave like you give, what would be our financial condition?
- If everyone handled conflict like you handle conflict, what sort of atmosphere would we enjoy?
- If everyone were the kind of Christian you are, what would be our community witness?

It is a vital key, a step in the process that cannot be overlooked—leaders have to be maturing, continuing in the process of growth! Replacing leaders who are not functioning properly is always painful. However, often such leaders are good people who have been placed in areas beyond their giftedness or maturity. Our motto is "Every member a minister." Different members minister at different levels, depending upon their level of commitment and maturity. Adult Sunday school teachers are required to develop and maintain a higher level of maturity than parking lot personnel. Why? They are leading more people. We cannot allow personalities, longevity, friendships, or other personal factors to determine the placement of leadership.

Component #7: Have Regular Leadership Meetings

On a periodic basis, leaders from every ministry should come together for a corporate time of vision casting, team building, and skill development. In addition, departments and ministries should also schedule regular meetings. This regular interaction provides several benefits.

VISION IS CONTINUALLY BEING UPDATED

Regular meetings with all ministry leaders give the senior pastor an opportunity to share the current vision for the church. Directions for the future can be shared, discussed, and developed. This gives the ministry leadership of the church an advance picture of the future. They can then begin to pray, plan, and program in accordance with the vision.

PROBLEMS ARE RESOLVED

Every church has difficulties. Many of the difficulties are the result of room sharing, scheduling conflicts, resource management, etc. By discussing problems in a corporate setting, every leader is allowed to participate in the decision making and subsequently support the conclusions.

A TEAM SPIRIT IS DEVELOPED

A football team is composed of various units and squads. The offensive line, the offensive backfield, the receivers, the defensive line, linebackers, defensive backfield, special teams, and kickers all have their own practices and drills. Still, on a regular basis the entire team practices together to ensure that each unit is operating in harmony with the others. On an effective team, every member of each unit understands and supports the others. An effective church team is similar to a football team. The pastor must understand the role of the nursery workers, the Sunday school teachers must support the parking lot personnel, the ushers must work together with the custodians. No team has ever won the Super Bowl without a unified team spirit. As the team prays, laughs, and cries together, it develops unity.

SKILLS ARE INTRODUCED AND IMPROVED

To continue to lead our people in growth, we ourselves must continue to grow. In leadership meetings, skills of conflict resolution, people management, teaching, and leading people are taught and developed.

DREAMS AND GOALS ARE SHARED

People love to dream! A big dream and its corresponding goals can inspire individuals to greater levels of service than they ever thought possible. The regular leadership meeting is the forum where we dream about new buildings, greater missions giving, or revolutionary new ministries. Often, as we dream aloud, God brings to light resources to help us achieve our dreams.

CORPORATE PRAYER IS OFFERED

There is power in agreement! As we take our individual and corporate needs to God in prayer, a divine energy is released. There is no better setting to pray for the needs of the church body than a leadership meeting.

Component #8: Prayer

Prayer alone will not build a great church, Sunday school class, or department. However, you cannot build a great church or class without prayer! The pastoral staff and the leadership team of the church must immerse every decision, program, and position in prayer. It is easy to place a personality, charmer, or wit in every position. But we want God's best for the church, the class, and the ministry. Sunday school superintendents should pray before asking anyone to teach the third-grade girls class. The third-grade girls teacher should pray before recruiting a helper or class secretary. The class secretary should pray each week for the absentees. Every member of the ministry team has a part in the prayer strategy. We can believe God to produce disciples in our classes! We can believe God to produce teachers, leaders, and divine servants! We ask God to help us continue our personal growth process so we can continue to lead others.

Are We Programming for Maturity

The following evaluation will help determine if you are designing and maintaining ministries that are developing maturity in the lives of believers.

1. Is every leader able to accurately and succinctly state the vision of our church or ministry?
2. Is every program and ministry evaluated on a regular (at least biannual) basis?
3. Is the leadership team meeting regularly for instruction, information, and inspiration?
4. Do leaders understand what is expected from them and their ministry area?
5. Have we eliminated programs that are not in accordance with the vision of our church?
6. Does our leadership team model maturity in tithing, personal devotion, witnessing, and church attendance?
7. Are new leaders being produced on a regular basis?
8. Are the habits of a disciple being reproduced in the lives of the average church member?

Only by asking and answering hard questions like these can you hope to initiate, develop, and maintain programs producing maturity in your people.

8
Continuous Lifetime Maturity

Maturity is a process. A typical Christian over the course of a lifetime will experience periods of great growth and periods of what appears to be dormancy. This cycle of Christian growth can be compared to the cycle of physical growth. Infant growth seems to occur daily. After a week's absence, many parents have declared their baby has grown at least 3 inches! Children go through amazing growth spurts, growing through shoes and clothes in a matter of weeks. Such rapid growth does not continue. During the course of childhood, there are growth spurts and growth slowdowns. Approaching adulthood, the adolescent may do aerobics, work out, or run in order to continue growth. As adults we sometimes grow in places we would prefer not to; only with great effort do we continue to grow where it's recommended.

New Christians grow at an amazing rate. Why? The information is all new; everything, from Bible stories to Sunday school lessons to prayer seminars, is fresh and alive. Voraciously, new Christians consume as much information and inspiration as possible, growing in Christ daily. There is nothing more exciting than discipling new Christians and enjoying their wonderment and excitement. Later, the process of spiritual growth slows. Growth must become both planned and intentional. As one matures in Christ, the areas worked on may be smaller. The new Christian may be trying to quit drinking and swearing, and learning how to pray and read the Bible. The mature Christian may be learning a greater degree of tenderness, exploring God's perspective on pain, or fine-tuning an attitude. Regardless of the stage of spiritual development, every believer must continue to grow!

How do you know if you are still growing? By evaluation. If growth is to be intentional, we must assess its progress to ensure that we are continuing to grow. The following questions will help you evaluate your personal spiritual growth over the last year.

IS YOUR LOVE EVIDENT TO OTHERS?

The disciples did not wear emblazoned T-shirts proclaiming them as disciples. They had no advertising, no television commercials, and no shoe contracts. In today's society, the disciples would attempt to renegotiate their contract to ensure a higher degree of visibility. But Jesus did teach them a way they could be identified. In essence, Jesus told them, "Guys, if you want people to know that you are associated with me, show them love and show love to each other." The disciples may have been disappointed that there was not a more exciting, glamorous way to be identified with Jesus. Loving people seemed so ordinary.

Love was the mark of discipleship then, and love is the mark of discipleship now. If you are growing, your love for others is increasing. If your love for others is not increasing, you are probably not growing! This year have you shown love to people that the world considers unlovable? Do others characterize you as loving and kind? At church, on the job, and in your family, do the people around you know that you love them? Is your love visible, evident, demonstrated in both words and actions? If you are not sure of the answer, ask the people around you!

Are the Habits of a Disciple Evident in Your Life and Increasing in Importance?

In the last year have you continued the five primary habits of a disciple? Do you spend time every day in the Bible? If you are in a growth mode, God will be revealing new and exciting things to you through the empowerment of the Holy Spirit. A mature believer eagerly anticipates time in the Word.

Do you spend time every day in prayer? Are you spending more time than you were last year? In order for your relationship with God to continue to progress, you must be spending daily time in fellowship with Him. This is not an option! If you are not praying, you are not growing!

Are you tithing to your local church? Do you enjoy giving, or has it become a chore? The growing believer is giving more and enjoying it more than ever before.

Are you attending church regularly? Do you attend Sunday school, Sunday morning, Sunday and Wednesday evenings?

Are you witnessing to others? In the last 12 months have you led anyone to Jesus or invited anyone to church? A growing disciple will produce other disciples. Our excitement about Jesus should always be evident to others.

Are You More Sensitive to God's Voice Than Ever Before?

This question deals with your spiritual sensitivity. Growing believers are aware that God can speak to them through His Word, through the Holy Spirit, through others, and through impressions. Are you asking God for and receiving His insight into situations and individuals? Your antenna should always be up and ready to receive from Him.

Are You Hungrier for God Than Ever Before?

This question deals with desire. "As the deer pants for water, so I long for you, O God" (Psalm 42:1, *The Living Bible*). This is a wonderful word picture of desire for God. Do you hunger for God that strongly?

Paul is a great example of someone who continued in his hunger for God. He said, "I want to know Christ" (Philippians 3:10). This was Paul, a man who had done great things for God. Why would he need to know Christ? Paul wanted to continue growing in his knowledge of Jesus. Are you as excited about knowing Jesus as you've ever been?

IS THE QUALITY OF FORGIVENESS EVIDENT IN YOUR LIFE?

Ouch! This is the question many people would prefer to skip. Forgiveness is not natural; it is supernatural. But mature believers are willing to forgive others in the same way Christ forgave them. John F. Kennedy once said, "Forgive your enemies, but remember their names." That is not God's idea of forgiveness! We must forgive completely, as we have been forgiven. Are you harboring bitterness toward someone who has wronged you? Are you unwilling to release a hurt that has occurred? Are there people in your workplace, your church, or your family that you have refused to forgive? Unforgiveness will stop your spiritual growth. It is a barrier we erect that keeps us from a complete relationship with Christ.

DO YOU HAVE A PLAN FOR GROWTH?

You will not grow without a plan. Remember that growth is intentional, not accidental! Each year you should chart your path for spiritual growth in the coming year. For many people this is the primary reason they do not grow. They have the desire to grow and the time to grow. But they neglect to plan for growth. Consequently, upon evaluating their year, they find that little, if any, growth has occurred. Hoping to grow spiritually without a plan is like trying to learn a new language without a teacher. What should constitute a growth plan? It can address spiritual growth, relational growth, physical growth, and personal growth. It should be established through careful evaluation and prayer.

A young man, age 30, developed the following plan. "Over the next 12 months, I intend to do the following:

- Read the Bible completely through at least two times.
- Spend a minimum of 30 minutes a day in prayer.
- Read at least 25 books to promote my biblical knowledge and spiritual development.
- Give more to God and missions than ever before.
- Attend Sunday, Wednesday, and special services held at my church.
- Disciple at least three people to a deeper relationship with Jesus.
- Lead at least one person a month to Jesus.
- Meet with my pastor quarterly to establish accountability and to review my progress.
- Spend more time with my wife and children.
- Establish a regular exercise program.
- Become more sensitive to the needs of others.
- Become a better worshiper."

With a plan like that, this young man will probably grow!

ARE YOU FOLLOWING YOUR GROWTH PLAN?

For a plan to be effective, it must be followed. This question deals with self-discipline. Are you on track with your plan in the areas where you felt God was challenging you to grow?

ARE YOUR SPIRITUAL AUTHORITIES AWARE OF AND INVOLVED IN YOUR GROWTH?

Your growth will be enhanced by the involvement of your Sunday school teacher, pastor, and spiritual leaders. Accountability is important to growth. Sometimes you may see little if any spiritual progress in yourself while others may see a great deal. At other times you may feel like you are right on track, without realizing you're ignoring a glaring area of weakness. Determine to be vulnerable with others and allow them to assist you in your growth.

DOES THE WORD OF GOD GOVERN YOUR LIFE HABITS?

This question deals with behavior. Are your actions consistent with God's commands? Is your flesh winning the battle for control of your habits? If you are growing, your habits should be conforming to His Word more and more. Will we all continue to struggle in some areas? Of course! Paul did. He wrote, "I do not understand what I do. For what I want to do I do not do, but what I hate I do" (Romans 7:15).

ARE YOU BECOMING MORE CHRISTLIKE IN YOUR THOUGHTS, ATTITUDES, AND BEHAVIORS?

Simply put, are you less like the world and more like Jesus? Is your Christlikeness increasing? This question speaks to the primary goal of Christianity: to be like Jesus! Each year, you should be more like Jesus than you have ever been before.

What Next?

We will never reach a place of perfect maturity until we reach heaven. But our maturity is for a purpose. We do not grow in Christ for growth's sake alone. Our growth is not part of some celestial contest whereby God proclaims a winner of the "Most Mature Award." Instead, our growth should propel us to the next level—ministry! The natural outgrowth of maturity is ministry.

You have been growing! You are now ready to assume a place of service in the local church. The question has now changed from How do I grow? to Where do I serve? For many Christians, this decision is difficult. The *We Build People* program has the following formula for determining a place of ministry. First Assembly of God in North Little Rock, Arkansas, has found it effective for placing hundreds of people.

The formula is Rick Warren's S.H.A.P.E. model. Job told God, "Your hands shaped me and made me" (Job 10:8). God has created you for a specific purpose. He shaped you and created you with your own unique gifts, talents, temperament, and abilities. Discover your area of maximum effectiveness as you consider the following:

S—SPIRITUAL GIFT

What is your spiritual gift? The spiritual gift that God has placed in your life will help determine your ministry niche. The gifts of administration, teaching, hospitality, pastoring, etc., all qualify a person for different areas of service. But even the most gifted become unhappy and ineffective serving in an area without the appropriate gift. For example, what happens when people with the gift of mercy and giving become business administrators? They give away the farm. They are unable to enforce policy and regulate spending. It's not their gift. A business administrator should have the gift of administration. People are fulfilled when they serve in their areas of giftedness.

H—HEART

What is your passion? What do you love to do? If your gift is teaching and you love four-year-olds, put them together. You will never be completely fulfilled teaching senior adults. If you're uncomfortable with infants, don't volunteer to work in the nursery. God speaks to us through our desires. God wants us to be happy and fulfilled in our service.

A—ABILITY

What is your ability? What do you do well? If you can't sing, don't try to join the choir. Everybody has special abilities. Instead of desiring the abilities of others, be content with the innate abilities that God has placed in you.

P—PERSONALITY

What is your personality? Some people are outgoing, others are shy. Some people are emotional, others are not. Find an area of ministry that matches your personality. Certain personalities are best suited for people ministries. Other personalities are best suited for procedure ministries. People ministries require relationship skills, warmth, empathy, good communication. Procedure ministries require detail, analysis, structure, concrete thinking. Outgoing people make great greeters, ushers, hostesses, and receptionists. They are not as well suited to be bookkeepers, soundmen, and media directors. Find a ministry that suits your personality.

E—EXPERIENCE

What is your experience? What have you done before? Your educational, spiritual, vocational, and even your painful experiences all prepare you for your ministry assignment. God will allow you to serve in an area you have had training and experience in. For instance, a career truck driver makes a great church bus driver. A carpenter is invaluable in constructing sets for drama presentations. A public school teacher is wonderfully trained to teach Sunday school.

People are most effective when they are fulfilling the purpose God has "shaped" them for. Your S.H.A.P.E. will help you determine your area of ministry. However, your ministry becomes more significant when you are dependent upon the Holy Spirit, the Master Teacher.

Conclusion

God has a purpose for you! Regardless of your present position on the growth scale, God wants to use you. As you commit yourself to spiritual growth and maturity, ask God to open your eyes to opportunities for ministry. Church members who have a place of ministry are more fulfilled, happy, and dedicated.

Resolve today to grow in God! There are no shortcuts to maturity. The path to Christlikeness requires determination, dedication, discipline, desire, devotion, and divine enablement. Henry Wadsworth Longfellow wrote:

The heights by great men reached and kept
Were not attained by sudden flight,
But they, while their companions slept,
Were toiling upward in the night.

Endnotes

[1]Bruce Wilkinson, *The Seven Laws of the Learner* (Sisters, Ore.: Multnomah Press, 1992), 124–25.

[2]Rick Warren, adapted from *The Purpose-Driven Church* (Grand Rapids: Zondervan Publishing House, 1995), 332–33.

[3]Gary J. Oliver, *How To Get It Right After You've Gotten It Wrong* (Wheaton, Ill.: Victor Books, Scripture Press, 1995), 137–38.

[4]Stuart Briscoe, *Discipleship for Ordinary People* (Wheaton, Ill.: Harold Shaw Publisher, 1995), 16–17.

[5]Mike Murdock, *101 Wisdom Keys* (Dallas: Wisdom International, 1994), 13.

[6]Michael M. Smith, ed., *Discipleship Journal*, July/Aug. 1997, 61.

[7]H. B. London, Jr., "The Pastor's Weekly Briefing" (Colorado Springs, Colo.: Focus on the Family), 1, September 5, 1997.

[8]Mike Murdock, *Dream Seeds* (Dallas: Widsom International), 100–01.

[9]Briscoe, *Discipleship for Ordinary People*, 194–95.

[10]*Discipleship Journal*, 66.

[11]Bobb Biehl, adapted from *Mentoring, Confidence in Finding a Mentor and Becoming One* (Nashville: Broadman and Holman Publishers, 1996), 29–30.

[12]Rod Loy, "Avoiding Staff Infection," *Enrichment*, General Council of the Assemblies of God, Summer 1997, 29–30.

[13]James M. Kouzes and Barry Z. Posner, *Credibility* (San Francisco: Jossey-Bass Publishers, 1993), 31.

[14]Ibid., 32.

[15]Ibid., 25.

[16]Jim Dethmer, adapted from "Moving in the Right Circles," *Leader-ship Journal*, vol.XIII, no.4, 86–91.

[17]Rick Warren, adapted from *Dynamic Bible Study Methods* (Wheaton, Ill.: Victor Books, Scripture Press, 1989), 34–36.

[18]Quiet time principles adapted from sermons by Alton Garrison, Mike Goldsmith, Mike Murdock, and Rick Warren.

[19]J. Robert Clinton, *The Making of a Leader: Recognizing the Stages of Leadership Development* (Colorado Springs, Colo.: NavPress, 1988), 14.

[20]Don Shula and Ken Blanchard, *Everyone's a Coach: You Can Inspire Anyone to Be a Winner* (Grand Rapids: Zondervan Publishing House, 1995), 85.

[21]Ibid., 121–22.

[22]Stephen Covey, *Principle-Centered Leadership* (Worthington, Ohio: Summit Books, 1991), 246.

[23]Oliver, 134–135.

[24]Shula and Blanchard, 30.

[25]George Barna, *Turning Vision Into Action* (Ventura, Calif.: Regal Books, 1996), 71.

[26]H. Norman Wright, *Communication Keys to Your Marriage* (Ventura, Calif.: Regal Books, 1974), 169.

[27]Bruce Wilkinson, *The 7 Laws of the Learner* (Sisters, Ore.: Multnomah Press, 1992), 288–89.

[28]Howard G. Hendricks, *The Seven Laws of the Teacher* (Portland, Ore.: Multnomah Press, 1987), 81.

[29]Ibid., 82–83.

[30]John Maxwell, "Keep on Keeping On…Consistency." An Injoy Life Lesson; audiotape.